The RS-232
Solution

The RS-232 Solution

Joe Campbell

Berkeley • Paris • Düsseldorf • London

Cover art by Patrice Larue
Drawings and technical illustrations by Lisa Amon
Layout and design by Ingrid Owen

BLACK BOX Catalog is a registered trademark of BLACK BOX Corp.
BLUEBOX is a trademark of International Data Sciences
Colonial Data and SB80 are registered trademarks of Colonial Data Services Corp.
CP/M is a registered trademark of Digital Research, Inc.
Diablo is a registered trademark of Xerox Corp.
Epson is a trademark of Epson America, Inc.
IBM is a registered trademark of International Business Machines
IBM Personal Computer is a trademark of IBM
INMAC is a trademark of Inmac Corp.
KayPro is a trademark of Non-Linear Systems Corp.
M.I.T.E. is a trademark of Mycraft Labs, Inc.
Mountain Computer is a trademark of Mountain Computers, Inc.
Northstar (Advantage) is a trademark of Northstar Computers, Inc.
Osborne is a trademark of Osborne Corp.
Smartmodem is a trademark of Hayes Microcomputer Products
Spinwriter is a registered trademark of NEC Corp.
Syzygy is a trademark of Syzygy Computer
Telenet is a service mark of G.T.E. Corp.
Tymnet is a sevice mark of G.E. Co.
Votrax is a trademark of Federal Screw Works (Type 'n Talk is a trademark of Votrax)
WordStar is a trademark of MicroPro International Corp.

SYBEX is not affiliated with any manufacturer.

Every effort has been made to supply complete and accurate information. However, SYBEX assumes no responsibility for its use, nor for any infringements of patents or other rights of third parties which would result.

Copyright©1984 SYBEX Inc., 2344 Sixth Street, Berkeley, CA 94710. World rights reserved. No part of this publication may be stored in a retrieval system, transmitted, or reproduced in any way, including but not limited to photocopy, photograph, magnetic or other record, without the prior agreement and written permission of the publisher.

Library of Congress Card Number: 83-51568
ISBN 0-89588-140-3
Printed in the United States of America
10 9 8 7 6 5 4 3 2

To Blossom

ACKNOWLEDGMENTS

I would like to thank: Cynthia Campbell for everything; Joel Klutch for his nit-picking review of the manuscript and the interfacing cases; David Haverty for the benefit of his experience; Steve Strand for his patience; Ben and Aaron Campbell for their tolerance.

Thanks to the entire SYBEX staff for its gracious support, especially Carole Alden, who must have found me insufferable during the early stages of editing. A tip of the hat also to Chris Mockel, Joel Kreisman, and Connie Gatto. Dianne Brock deserves credit for coaxing me to SYBEX in the first place.

A large amount of the credit should go to Rudolph Langer, the SYBEX Editor-in-Chief. His enthusiasm, generosity, and trust were inspirational.

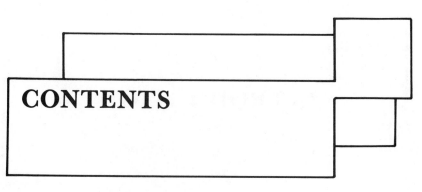

CONTENTS

INTRODUCTION

Nothing in the world of microcomputers is more reviled, despised, or misunderstood than the RS-232-C interface. Ordinarily mild-mannered humans are driven berserk by the experience of connecting their computer equipment. Sometimes this rage gets out of hand:

> A dispute between a customer and a computer store over a $180 bill has ended in tragedy with the fatal shooting of the store's owner.
>
> A 42-year-old man, Floyd French of Gladstone, Missouri, was arrested at the scene and later charged with first-degree murder. The victim was the owner of the Altair Computer Center, Henry Phillip Bouldin. According to police, French had bought a computer from Bouldin, then brought in a printer purchased elsewhere and asked that [the store] make the two compatible...
>
> —*InfoWorld*, June 20, 1983

A computerist purchases a microcomputer with an "RS-232-C compatible" serial interface, and later purchases a well-known printer. When the the two units are connected by a standard *EIA RS-232-C full-duplex cable,* not only does the printer refuse to print, it also paralyzes the computer.

The owner hopefully contacts the manufacturer of the printer, who replies:

> There are over 100,000 copies of our product in use in 45 countries. Our interface, by virtue of its numbers, is a proven standard. We recommend you contact the

maker of your computer and ask him what steps are necessary to bring its interface into conformity with standard practices.

Disconsolate, the owner writes the manufacturer of his computer, who reassures him:

> Our technical manual should provide to a qualified technician all the information necessary to successfully connect our product to any RS-232-C interface. Enclosed you will find an order form on which I have filled in the part number for the technical manual. If you will return it with a check for $45, I'll personally see to it that your manual goes out by return mail.

The beleaguered owner, having already spent slightly more on the printer than he could afford, is now facing an additional $45 charge for a book from which he will have to pay a technician another $45 to extract a single fact or two. To these costs will eventually be added $35 for a custom cable. "Oh, well," he thinks, "at least there is the consolation that more than 100,000 souls in 45 countries share my suffering."

There is, of course, no guarantee that a technician or even an engineer will succeed in solving this interface problem. It is not uncommon for professional hardware designers to flounder badly when trying to decipher an interface of someone else's design. For example, one of the most prolific designers on the micro scene today describes his experiences with routine RS-232-C interfacing:

> Among the most exasperating experiences in any computer user's career is connecting two serial devices. I don't mean a terminal and a modem— making that connection is a piece of cake—but any other connection can be real trouble. For instance, every time I buy a new piece of equipment, things seem to go this way: I spend five minutes reading the sales brochure, five minutes executing the financial transaction, and five hours trying to figure out how to make the new equipment communicate with my computer.
>
> —"Ciarcia's Circuit Cellar," *BYTE,* April 83

What *is* an RS-232-C and why is it responsible for so much misery? The RS-232-C interface is the chief means by which auxiliary microcomputer equipment is interconnected. Although it derives from a very rigid standard (**R**ecommended **S**tandard number **232**, revision **C** from the Electronic Industry Association), virtually every manufacturer takes broad liberties with it. The purpose of any standard is to prevent confusion, so it is ironic that the use of a standard should promulgate confusion.

Most of the difficulties associated with RS-232-C stem from its being ill-suited to the tasks for which it is commonly employed. As we shall see in Chapter 2, the standard itself was devised to solve a very specific interfacing problem—modems to terminals. The manufacturers of micros and peripherals, anxious for compatibility with a wide range of equipment, understandably turned to the well-known and reliable RS-232-C. But because they were immediately faced with interfacing situations not covered by the rules set down in the standard, designers were forced to adapt the rules to fit the requirements of the interface.

The problems generated by this fundamental incompatibility are exacerbated by what has now become a "design by rumor" approach to interface design. This process is not unlike the parlor game in which a player writes down a story and whispers it to a neighbor, who tells a neighbor, and so on. When each player has told the story, the last player recounts the tale. The story has been wildly transformed in the retelling. This is a study in psychology, how personality inevitably interferes with one's perception of the truth. A similar process has occurred with the RS-232-C standard: designers and writers have relied upon the secondhand interpretations of others. In this way, interfacing irregularities established in a single, popular computer product are often perpetuated as other manufacturers scurry to maintain compatibility with it.

The upshot of these difficulties is that microcomputer versions of the RS-232-C interface have become intellectually unwieldy. Anyone who wants to interface microcomputers can look to the official standard for only the broadest of guidelines.

When an elephant flies, it shouldn't be criticized for doing it badly. Despite its myriad flavors, micro interfacing remains manifestly understandable. The goal of this book is to distill what is useful and meaningful from the RS-232-C standard, mix it with a few parts of experience, add a dash of common sense, then serve it up in the form of examples.

The most important aim is to impart not just the abstract knowledge required to understand abstract interfacing problems, but also a working methodology for actually building a functioning cable for any two "RS-232-C compatible" devices. So this is both a "how it works" and a "how to work it" book.

It would be unfair to claim that computer experience is unnecessary for mastering this subject. This is not a book for beginners, an "Idiot's Guide to Interfacing." Readers are assumed to possess some knowledge of computer concepts. While we do not presuppose an ability to program in any specific language, the concepts and problems are more easily understood if you know what programming is. Likewise, a *user's* knowledge of some operating system—such as CP/M, MS-DOS, PC-DOS, or TRS-DOS—is necessary to understand the problems and the procedures required to solve them.

Interfacing has been relegated to the technician and engineer long enough. The air of black magic and mystery that surrounds it must be blown away once and for all. No special technical skills are required to follow the ideas and examples contained here. This is a frequent and usually perfunctory claim. Books on technical subjects sometimes lure you with one or two simple-minded chapters, then abruptly slam you into a wall of technical jargon and obfuscation. Here you do *not* have to know anything about electronics or about circuitry. No voltmeters or oscilloscopes. You don't even have to solder.

Still, the very fact that you have purchased a book on so recondite a subject as RS-232-C interfacing suggests that you are probably not terrified at the prospect of manipulating a wire or handling connectors and cables, and that you don't break into a sweat upon looking at the rear of a computer. If this doesn't describe you, don't abandon hope, just proceed more slowly.

In Chapter 1, "The Interface," we discuss the very idea of an interface, why it exists and what it must accomplish. We quickly review such terms as bit (serial) and byte (parallel). We trace the historical origins of serial data transfer and the evolution of a set of circumstances that eventually led to the adoption of a serial interface standard. We see why the microcomputer industry adopted the RS-232-C interface even in the face of its obvious unsuitability and problems of compatibility.

In Chapter 2, "Interfacing Basics," we take up concepts basic to all RS-232-C interfacing. Here you discover that all RS-232-C devices can be divided into two basic categories. For the first time you begin to learn

the names of the various pins and signals and to analyze their customary uses. You discover that, depending upon which category of device
you're considering, the roles (but *not* the names) of the pins will change.
You are introduced to the idea of *handshaking*—one piece of equipment
controlling another through the interchange of electrical signals and the
manipulation of the voltage levels on various pins. In one form or
another, the process of handshaking is the principle idea in much of this
book. At the end of Chapter 2, the chameleon term "RS-232-C compatibility" is discussed. Here you will find an enumeration of the few
areas of agreement among microcomputer interfaces.

In Chapter 3, "The UART: Elves in the Basement," we suspend
our discussion of the actual RS-232-C interface in order to learn
exactly *how* one device is able to control another. To this end, we
develop a conceptual model of a real device – the UART (Universal
Asynchronous **R**eceiver-**T**ransmitter). Applying the ideas derived in
the previous chapter to this model, we gradually add functions and
pins, showing each's role in the interface. Toward the end of this chapter, we return to the interface with a new understanding of device control. You are then introduced to such practical considerations as the
inner working of print buffers and the differences between software
and hardware handshaking. By the end of Chapter 3, you will have an
understanding of what is required to interface a printer. Best of all,
you will have learned all the pin names and numbers you will need in
order to understand the case studies in later chapters.

Chapter 4, "Tricks and Flips," is subtitled "Coping With The Real
World." Since you will encounter few "standard" RS-232-C devices,
this chapter teaches you how to deal with workaday problems such as
missing outputs, sex incompatibilites, and oddball configurations.
Chapter 4 ends with a summary of the functions of the **BIG EIGHT**,
the eight most important pins on the interface.

If anything in this book can be called technical, it is Chapter 5,
"Logic Levels." These are the details required in order to understand
the testing procedure we will develop in the next chapter. Topics such
as logic inversion, noise margin, and transition regions are treated.
Here we also establish an unambiguous vocabulary for talking about
the relationship between voltage levels and logic levels. How long can
an RS-232-C cable be? This is one of the practical questions answered
in this chapter.

In Chapter 6, "The Interfacer's Toolkit," we construct a simple set of tools consisting of three custom connectors, two ordinary cables, two 15¢ light-emitting diodes, and a half-dozen solderless connectors known as grabbers. The total price of the entire kit (less the cables, which you may have lying around) is about $12. When you make your first 3-wire cable (instead of purchasing $30–$50 custom cables) for less than $5, you will have reimbursed yourself not only for the toolkit, but for the price of this book as well.

The second section of this chapter, "Step-by-Step Interfacing," is the denouement that we've been building toward. Here we set out the simple, 5-step strategy we'll apply in all our case studies.

Chapter 7 is "Case Study 1: SB80/ADDS." In this first case study, we honor the faithful terminal and computer used to write this book. They pose a good beginning study because they have simple device control and they need no handshaking. The primary goals of this chapter will be to learn how to use the tools, how to follow the procedures for testing, and how to make a logic chart. As in all case studies, we end with a few comments and a recipe for making a cable.

Computer manuals are frequently misleading, misinformed, or downright incorrect when it comes to their RS-232-C interfaces. With this in mind, our interfacing techniques don't rely on documentation of any kind. At the end of a case study, however, we may review the manufacturers' literature (perhaps giving them a tweak on the nose) in order to illustrate how widespread and severe are the misconceptions about the RS-232-C interface.

In Chapter 8, "Case Study 2: N*/OKI," we undertake to interface a Northstar Advantage computer and an Okidata Microline 83A printer. This is our first real encounter with handshaking, so a foolproof method of locating the handshaking signals is developed.

Chapter 9, "Case Study 3: KayPro/Epson," is subtitled "The Case of the Intermittent Printer." We try to solve a mysterious problem between these two popular pieces of microcomputer equipment. The problem has been made more interesting by the tampering of a "knowledgeable friend." The outcome illustrates some important pointers about handshaking.

Chapter 10, "Case Study 4: OSB/TNT," is also a mystery, one that almost ends in a "deadly embrace" between the actors. This time, one of the protagonists has a bad reputation for talking back to would-be interfacers.

Chapter 11, "Case Study 5: IBM/NEC," spotlights the ubiquitous

IBM Personal Computer and NEC Spinwriter, a popular letter-quality printer. Many people have complained that letter-quality printers are hard to interface. As you will see, there's nothing to it.

The modem occupies a special place in the topic of RS-232-C interfacing. Chapter 12, "Interfacing Modems," is a mini-primer on how modems work, followed by three case studies. The last two studies show how software can dramatically alter the personality of an RS-232-C interface.

Our last, Chapter 13, "Professional Tools," surveys and reviews some handy tools and gadgets for those who take their interfacing seriously. Photos, prices, and addresses are included.

Questions or comments about this book may be directed to the author by electronic mail: THE SOURCE #STN984 CompuServe #74105,1632.

Part I

THE INTERFACE

1

Since a computer is designed to be a logical device, we seldom even think of the physical manifestations behind its logical concepts. Indeed, contemplation of what is taking place inside the computer sometimes actually obscures a topic by adding a superfluous layer of complexity. For example, it is common knowledge that *logical* data in microcomputers is represented as *bits* (binary digits). Bits are customarily explained through tables that illustrate each bit's contribution to some overall logical scheme.

DATA TRANSFER MODES

Although the bit is an intellectual construction, it is, nevertheless, *physically* a voltage whose magnitude gives the bit its value (i.e, one or zero). The electrical current that represents computer data is no different from that found in a stereo set where electrical impulses are transported from point to point via wires. When bits must be moved about within the computer itself, they are transmitted along wires just as any other voltage. If the data to be transmitted is in 8-bit format *bytes*—as it usually is in microcomputers—then eight separate, discrete wires must simultaneously carry the eight representative electrical currents between the two points. A quick glimpse inside your computer will illustrate this arrangement: you will see row upon row of etched wires running side by side among the integrated circuits and other components on the circuit boards.

This simultaneous transmission of the eight bit-voltages that constitute a byte is referred to as *parallel* transfer. Parallel transfer, then, is done byte-by-byte. Since all eight bits arrive at their destination at the same instant, parallel data transfer can be accomplished at extremely high speeds. These qualities make it the the preferred method of data transfer whenever possible. Figure 1.1 illustrates this simple concept.

Data transfer, especially high-speed data transfer, demands a tightly controlled environment. The internal temperature of the computer must be regulated and the electrical properties of resistance, capacitance, and inductance carefully calculated. As long as data is being moved about *inside* a computer, this environment is stable and predictable. But a great deal of computer data must be transported to a potentially hostile *outside* world. In fact, the commercial success of a microcomputer is often directly related to the effectiveness with which it moves data to and from *peripheral devices* such as printers, terminals, speech synthesizers, modems, print buffers, etc. The transfer of data

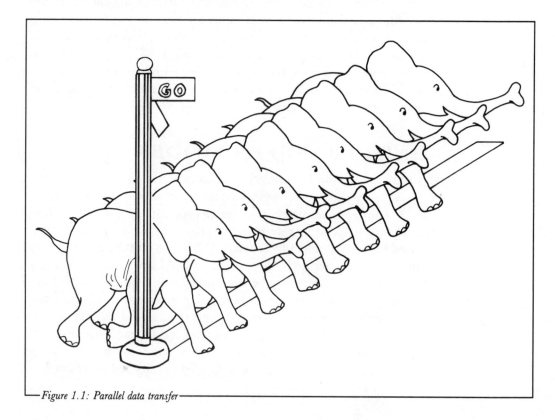

Figure 1.1: Parallel data transfer

from a computer to an outside device is known as *output;* conversely, data transferred from an external device into the computer is *input.* These processes are known collectively as *input/output,* or simply *I/O.*

THE INTERFACE

If a computer's internal environment is considered to be an accommodating one, then outside the computer is Chaos. From a design standpoint, absolutely nothing may be assumed about the environmental conditions the data will suffer outside the hospitable environs of the computer itself. The problem posed by this situation is simply stated: how can we extract data from circuitry so sensitive that the mere addition of an extra length of wire—or even a change in the position of existing wires—can upset the delicate electrical balance required to sustain operation? How can we immunize our computer's delicate innards against someone's well-intentioned attempt to "computerize" a doorbell or a toaster? In other words, we must somehow ensure that deleterious events outside the computer will not be allowed to harm the computer's circuitry; we need an *interface,* the point of contact between dissimilar environments. Since an interface is a sort of "door" to the computer's world, it is sometimes called an *I/O port,* or just a *port.*

A familiar example of an interface is the one between our homes and the local power company. The power company transports electrical energy in the form of an extremely high voltage. It would be imprudent to bring 100,000 volts into the home of the consumer—a surefire method of depleting the customer base. Therefore, as the first step of interfacing with home appliances, these high-voltage lines are reduced to safer levels. The power company (with the cooperation of local codes and Public Utilities Commissions) also dictates the requirements for public connection to the power transfer system. Before power can be connected, the power company must inspect the building site to make certain that its wiring conforms to the prescribed interface. In this example, the interface serves a triple purpose: first, it prevents damage to the power company's distribution system; second, it prevents consumer self-incineration; third, it provides a reasonable combination of safety and usability.

Self-protection is only one of the goals for any interface; the primary objective is, after all, to provide a medium for the transfer of data. The last point—usability—is also important. If self-protection is achieved at the expense of usability, the interface will be neither accommodating nor inviting. It is comparatively easy to design a circuit that cannot easily be damaged by external abuse, but real skill is required to make it also easy to use, even for the uninitiated.

Once such an interface has been established, the transfer of data to external environments is possible. Unfortunately, new problems arise almost immediately. The first is an obvious one: if the data must be transferred a long distance, the cost in wire becomes significant. For parallel transfers, at least nine wires—eight for the data bits, one for circuit common ("ground")—are needed. Still more wires are usually required to control the flow of data across the interface. Anyone who has ever built a full-blown parallel interface cable will attest that dealing with its 30 or so wires is expensive, cumbersome, and tedious. Another problem associated with parallel data transfer lies in the very nature of the bit/voltages themselves. When a bit/voltage changes state from a one to a zero, or vice versa, it does so very rapidly—in the order of *nanoseconds* (one billionth of a second). This abruptness is itself an essential part of the process of data transfer. Slow changes between zero and one are not even recognized as data. Unfortunately, as a cable gets longer, its electrical properties (capacitance and inductance) restrict the abruptness with which a bit can change between zero and one, and data corruption or loss becomes likely. Because of this, the speed inherent in parallel data transfers makes transmission over long cables problematical.

These dual impediments to parallel data transfer—expense and data degradation—restrict its use to a few peripheral devices (such as printers) that are likely to be used in close proximity to the computer, or that must operate at very high speeds. Because no long cables are required, it remains the data transfer method of choice for internal computer use.

A more rugged, less expensive method of data transfer is clearly needed. To be a competitive alternative, though, it must offer substantial improvements in cost and bulk, while preserving data integrity.

The obvious alternative to sending all bits simultaneously on multiple wires is to send them singly, one after the other. At the receiving end, the process is reversed and the individual bits are reassembled into the original byte. With just one bit to transmit at a time, data can be transferred with a simple electrical circuit consisting of only two wires. This scheme—known as *serial* transfer—reduces the bulk and much of the expense of the parallel technique.

Unfortunately, this savings is offset by a decrease in efficiency: it takes at least eight times longer to transmit eight individual bits one after the other than to transmit them all simultaneously in parallel. Luckily, this speed loss does not prove to be a significant limitation in most applications. If we look at some typical serial peripheral devices, we see an interesting common characteristic—they are inherently slow, at least in comparison to the internal speed of microprocessors. Each involves some time-consuming, usually mechanical process that greatly limits its speed: printers are limited by the speed of their print-heads, modems by the frequency restrictions of the telephone lines, and disk drives by their slow rotational speed. So the speed inherent in the process of parallel data transfer is largely wasted on such peripheral devices. The serial method, therefore, can afford to sacrifice some speed while still adequately servicing the peripheral devices. In such cases, the sacrifice in speed is inconsequential in comparison to the increased reliability and transmission range.

STANDARD INTERFACES

So far, we have established only that an interface is required between a computer and the outside world, and that it should transfer data serially. But, since there are always several ways to design any circuit "correctly," any number of perfectly functional interfaces for

Figure 1.2: Serial data transfer

an application are possible. In this diversity lies a problem fundamental to all interface circuitry: compatibility with other interfaces. A brief glimpse into the past will be helpful in understanding this problem.

Historically, the serial data interface has been quite diverse. Many of the ideas touched upon in this book date directly from the technology of the 19th century. Data has been transmitted intercontinentally since 1866. In fact, the dots and dashes of Morse code are the precursors to the zeros and ones used in computer data communication today. The rise to maturity of serial technology and the proliferaton of various teleprinter and teletypewriter devices inevitably led to a bewildering array of serial devices, each with its own interface. In electronic terms, the telegraph line is an unrefined medium, extremely tolerant of wide variations in the electrical characteristics of the equipment connected to it. Because it is very forgiving of abuse, designers of serial equipment could safely neglect some of the finer points of electrical design. In a sense, then, there existed no real motivation to develop a standard interface. The gradual insinuation of computers into the field of communications has provided that impetus. When computers arrived on the scene, teleprinter and teletype technology was already mature and well-defined (albeit primitive), so it is easy to see why they were naturally adopted as input/output devices.

Today when we visualize a computer, we see a person working at a keyboard and video display. But early computers were not operated in this manner; most input and output was done by punched cards or paper tape. However, as computers and their operating systems became more powerful, it became possible for them to interact directly with humans. Time-sharing systems, where several users are connected to a computer at the same time, became common. Soon it became economically desirable for the users to access computers from remote locations. Short distances—a few hundred feet, perhaps within the same building—could be spanned by the addition of extra wires. But the lure of *distant* remote access beckoned, and computer engineers began to ogle the telephone lines longingly. After all, the telephone company had already strung wires to almost everywhere . . . best of all, they were for rent cheaply!

For reasons we'll explore in Chapter 12, "Interfacing Modems," computer data cannot be injected directly into the telephone networks. A translating device—the *modem*—is required. When computerized telecommunications was in its infancy, the Bell System supplied most of the data equipment connected to its lines. Bell naturally exercised strict control over the modem interface. But as activity in the telecommunications field increased apace, and more and different kinds of equipment began to appear, Bell surveyed the hodgepodge of equipment that the computer industry was threatening to connect to its lines. It saw little that it liked and much that it felt would compromise and complicate the delivery of communications service to the public. The telephone companies predictably prohibited the connection of most of these devices.

Figure 1.3: Ma Bell eschews potential pluggers-in.

THE RS-232-C INTERFACE STANDARD

The situation cried for a standard, and it was not long in coming. In 1969 the EIA (Electronic Industries Association), Bell Laboratories, and manufacturers of communications equipment cooperatively formulated and issued the EIA RS-232, which almost immediately underwent minor revisions to become RS-232-C. A similar standard was issued by the international standards organization, Consultative Committee on International Telegraphy and Telephony (CCITT). In order for microcomputer users to understand this inherited standard, it must be emphasized that the RS-232-C interface was developed for a single purpose, unambiguously stated by its title:

> Interface Between Data Terminal Equipment and Data Communications Equipment Employing Serial Binary Data Interchange

Every word in the title is significant: it describes the interface between a *terminal* (Data Terminal Equipment, or DTE) to a *modem* (Data Communication Equipment, or DCE) for the transfer of serial data. The document consists of four parts.

- **Electrical Signal Characteristics** This describes the electrical "face" the interface will present to and require from the outside world. The voltage levels to represent logical 0 and 1 are defined here.
- **Interface Mechanical Characteristics (Connectors)** This section dictates that the interface must consist of a plug and a receptacle and that the receptacle will be on the DCE. The pin number assignments are specified, but, it should be noted, the exact connector itself is not. The familiar D-shaped *DB-25 connector,* now almost synonymous with the serial interfaces, derives from another standards body, The International Standards Organization, or ISO. The details of this connector are shown in Figure 1.4.
- **Functional Description of Interchange Circuits** This section defines and gives names to the functions of the electrical signals to be used. Here, for example, **TRANSMITTED DATA** is assigned to pin 2. There are 21 such definitions, but only a few of them are relevant to microcomputers.

- **Standard Interfaces for Selected Communications System Configurations** These are recipes for common kinds of modem-to-terminal connections.

How The RS-232-C Standard Applies To Micros

"OK," you say, "all this DCE/DTE stuff is grand, but where does it tell me how to hook up my RS-232-C compatible tape drive unit?"

Sorry, but nowhere.

"Well, how about my RS-232-C compatible printer?"

No, not that, either.

Actually, the true RS-232-C standard is largely ignored in, and irrelevant to, the world of microcomputers. Unless you have a "Bell compatible" modem to connect to a conventional dumb terminal, the standard will not be much help. You're on your own with everything else. Moreover, almost everyone who looks to the standard for explicit help finds it confusing, misleading, and suffocatingly technical. When using it for assistance in a typical interfacing problem—for example, a printer to a microcomputer—one is bombarded by pins whose names obviously have nothing to do with either a printer or a computer: "Ring Indicator" and "Received Line Signal Detector." Abandoning all hope of extracting sense from the standard itself, you turn to the

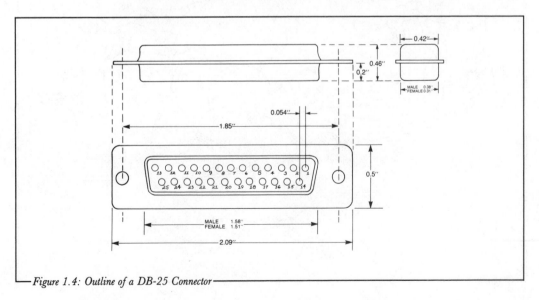

Figure 1.4: Outline of a DB-25 Connector

equipment manufacturers for illumination. None will be forthcoming: even so-called "end-user" manuals perpetuate the standard's obscure, forbidding terminology.

What's going on here? This is just an example of the old computer hide-and-seek: hardware and software designers stand on opposite sides of a problem and point accusingly at each other. The hardware manufacturers wish on the one hand to retain an advertising claim to "RS-232-C compatibility," but on the other hand candidly confess that strict observation of the standard on microcomputers is not practical. Meanwhile, software authors complain that they must customize the I/O sections of their programs for each different machine because of "incomplete or nonstandard implementation of the RS-232-C standard." Convincing arguments can be made for both sides.

This state of confusion is traceable directly to the attempt to adapt a complicated, highly specialized standard to applications for which it was never intended. Because of its complexity and the narrow range of

Figure 1.5

Since no suitable, generalized standard exists for interfacing serial devices, would we prefer that each manufacturer promiscuously concoct his own? Should the manufacturer of a $5000 (or $100, for that matter) micro really be criticized because the serial interface he fully expects will spend its life driving a Type 'n Talk doesn't fully implement the RS-232-C standard, or that it uses pins not defined in the standard? Sooner or later we must stop this childish complaining and get down to the business of getting everyone to agree on which of the pins are needed for the most common operations. We should leave a few undefined pins for the renegades to futz with. If this could be accomplished, an air of sanity and simplicity would descend over the subject and many common interface problems would dissolve.

the equipment it embraces, using the RS-232-C standard for ordinary microcomputer interfacing problems is a case of overkill.

Before you rush to a final judgment, however, there are some things to be said in defense of the much-maligned standard. By rescuing us from drowning in a sea of incompatible interfaces, the mere existence of *any* standard has, in a way, been a salvation for the microcomputer industry. Far from lamenting that manufacturers have not religiously adhered to a standard universally acknowledged to be inappropriate for most applications, we should instead rejoice that they have saved us from a stultifying entanglement in wires. Also keep in mind that rigorous standards frequently stifle invention as much as they purge inconsistencies and incompatibilities. And not all standards have the desired result. Witness the infamous EIA RS-234-C dealing with measurement of audio amplifier power. Inherently misleading and frequently abused by manufacturers' advertisements, the use of this standard in consumer advertising was eventually restricted by the Federal Trade Commission.

It is too easy to complain that computer manufacturers have abused the RS-232 standard. This view is unnecessarily harsh. In the absence of a formal standard explicitly designed for general-purpose serial interfacing, these manufacturers could easily have gone the way of other industries, each implementing his own *minimum* interface as necessary. Indeed, inexpensive "home" computers have done exactly this. On the contrary, the opposite has actually occurred among the mainstream of serious microcomputer manufacturers: they have opted for the relatively complicated RS-232-C interface where a less elaborate (and less expensive) one would have sufficed.

For better or worse, the RS-232-C standard is used by most major computer manufacturers. Nor is it likely to disappear. Even if the progenitor RS-232-C dies, its children will be around forever in the form of RS-232-C compatible devices. The EIA has seen to this in the new serial standards, RS-422-A and RS-423-A.

In this spirit, we will spend little time explaining how to connect the EIA intended modems and terminals for full logic control. Such stuff belongs in a different book. But, since the EIA standard actually *defines* the interface, we will not hesitate to draw from it. Yet our basic mission will always be to extract from the RS-232-C standard only the details that help us to understand the interfaces found and implemented on typical microcomputers and peripherals. As a practical matter, that ubiquitous D-shaped connector on your computer *is* the RS-232-C interface. You should come to view it as you would a standard screw thread, or perhaps an electrical outlet. That somewhere, in an earlier time, for a different reason, on different equipment, the connector was used for another purpose—these things to us will have no significance.

In this book we will take an entirely pragmatic approach to the transfer of data across the interface. We will largely ignore the data itself, so don't be concerned that you haven't the foggiest idea what constitutes data, or how it is actually transmitted or received. We are interested only in what is required to make the interface function, how the wires should be connected and what happens if they aren't. Purely as a matter of tutorial convenience, we'll pretend that if the wires are correctly connected, the data will magically move across the interface. In other words, we are going to treat the task of data transfer just as if we were moving a chain of slowly moving elephants across a drawbridge—the first step is to get the bridge down.

INTERFACING BASICS

2

In its simplest form, the RS-232-C interface consists of only two wires—one to carry data, plus a *circuit common*. The circuit common is often erroneously called "circuit ground." It has absolutely nothing to do with ground or earth. It is just the absolute voltage reference for all the interface circuitry, the point in the circuit from which all voltages are measured. The concept of circuit common is notoriously confusing, even to people accustomed to analyzing electronic circuits. We do not wish to let such parenthetical ideas get in the way of understanding how to get the interface to work. The only thing to remember is that this connection between pin 7's *must* be made on *every* RS-232-C connector no matter how simple or complex. It is one of the few true *universals*—just make the connection and forget about it.

In the example in Figure 2.1, we will begin by looking at a typical

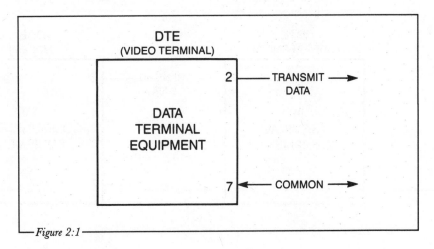

Figure 2:1

DTE device, an ordinary video terminal consisting of a keyboard and a video display. (The DTE/DCE distinction will soon become clear.) The numbers inside the boxes refer to the pin numbers on the connector.

When you first see the phrase **TRANSMIT DATA,** you may become uneasy that "transmission" has not been previously defined. Is the transmission electrical? Is it electromagnetic? How you view the process really doesn't matter. Most people's *intuitive* understanding of these terms is sufficient, so feel free to concoct your own model and substitute your own vocabulary. For example, you may elect to think of transmission/reception as "generation/detection" or as "origination/termination." You may even visualize outbound signals "coming out of " the transmitter while inbound signals "go into" the receiver.

It takes two devices to make an interface: the existence of transmitted data implies the presence of another device to receive the data being transmitted. In Figure 2.2, we will assume this device is the archetypal DCE device, a modem.

Look closely at the diagram—the transmitted data comes *out of* pin 2 of the DTE device, and goes *into* pin 2 of the DCE device. If transmitted data is arriving at a pin on the DCE, it is reasonable to assume that the DCE must therefore be *receiving* the same data. The label **TRANSMIT DATA,** then, does not belong between the devices: whether the data is transmitted or received depends entirely upon which device's perspective you look from. To clarify this relationship, let's temporarily put the labels *inside* the boxes representing the devices, as shown in Figure 2.3.

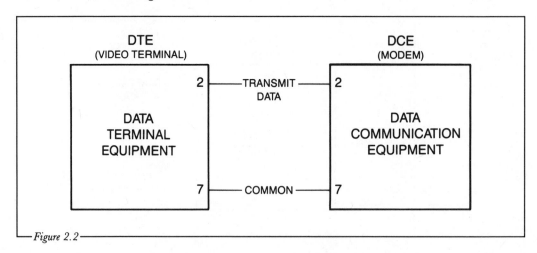

Figure 2.2

So data on pin 2 of the DTE is transmitted, while the same data on pin 2 of a DCE is received data. From here on, we may refer to an outbound (transmitted) signal as output, and that any inbound (received) signal as input. *Signal* is a general term loosely describing *all* electrical activity on the interface.

As in the previous example, names of inputs will be written in lowercase letters and marked with a **?**, while outputs are written in capital letters and marked with a **!**. This terminology will make it easier to maintain a visual image of what is actually happening and will help avoid ambiguity when describing the direction of data transfer. When the full signal name is used *in text* (as opposed to in a diagram), we will continue to write it entirely in capital letters. Remember, the **!** and **?** along with the upper/lowercase convention were invented especially for this book and are not part of any standard or even in general use elsewhere.

BIDIRECTIONAL DATA

Our hypothetical terminal transmits characters typed on its keyboard. A modem receives these characters and sends them down the phone line. Terminals and modems, however, are not usually one-way devices—each may also perform the opposite function. For example, modems usually fetch characters from the telephone line and output them to the terminal. Similarly, the terminal receives the characters output from the modem and displays them on the video screen. Both of our

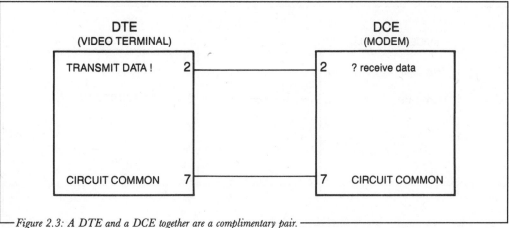

Figure 2.3: A DTE and a DCE together are a complimentary pair.

sample devices must therefore be able both to transmit *and* receive data, so let's add these new functions to our diagram in Figure 2.4.

In this example the data flow is a bidirectional interchange between the two devices. This is directly analogous to the connection of two telephones as shown in Figure 2.5.

It's time to deliver on the promise to pin down the differences between DTE and DCE devices. Here it is:

> DTEs transmit on pin 2 and receive on pin 3.
> DCEs transmit on pin 3 and receive on pin 2.

Complex notions are frequently oversimplified in order to illustrate fundamental relationships . . . this is not the case here. It really is that simple! No matter how elaborate an interface becomes, how many wires are involved, or how sophisticated the equipment being interfaced, your analysis of an interfacing problem will always begin by determining the direction of data flow on pins 2 and 3.

(In later serial standards the EIA says DTE stands for Data *Terminating* Equipment. The implication here is that a DCE is any device that passes data, while a DTE device is actually the terminus for the data. Since it may do both, a computer doesn't fit into either of these categories.)

HANDSHAKING

If things are so simple, you may ask, why are there 21 wires? Why has such a simple matter confounded so many bright people for so

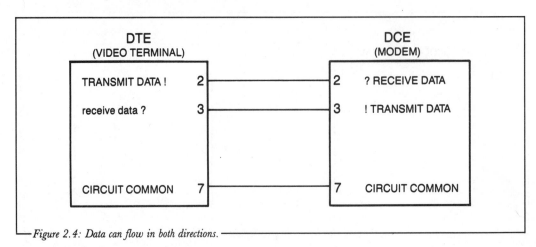

Figure 2.4: Data can flow in both directions.

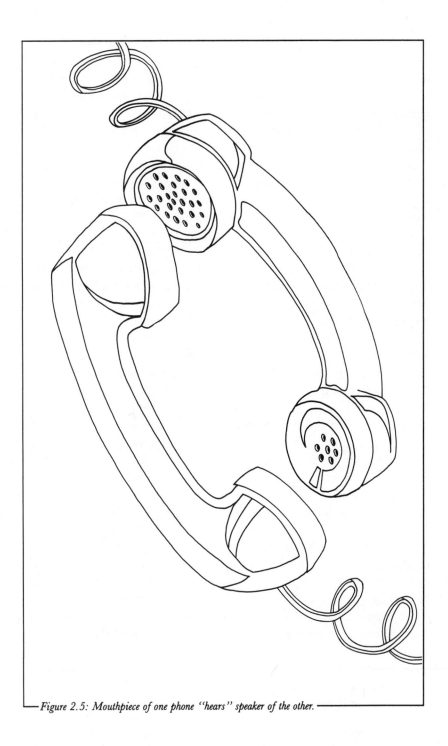

Figure 2.5: Mouthpiece of one phone "hears" speaker of the other.

long? Surely an entire book on such a simple topic is not required. To be sure, there is more to understanding the microcomputer's use of the interface. But not much more. There remains only the straightforward matter of *interactive device control*. This forbidding-sounding term is generally referred to by the less severe (and infinitely more suggestive of its function) term, *handshaking*. Handshaking is the way in which the data flow across the interface is regulated and controlled.

Although we will identify and discuss two distinct kinds of handshaking—*software handshaking* and *hardware handshaking*—we'll focus primarily on hardware handshaking. For purposes of comparison, however, a cursory discussion of software handshaking is called for here.

Software handshaking occurs when one device controls another by the *content* of the data. For example, one way to control a printer is by having the computer send its characters line-by-line. After each line, the computer automatically puts in a character saying to the printer "This is the end-of-line...I'm waiting for your signal to send the next line." The printer accepts the line, prints it, then sends a character back to the computer, meaning, "I'm ready for another line." This is an easy way to control a printer, but not all printers are able to recognize or respond to such *control characters* in the data stream.

By contrast, with hardware handshaking we are working at a more fundamental, in-case-of-fire-break-glass level where a printer can actually force the computer to pause in sending characters just by changing the voltage on a wire. It solves communication problems at the most basic hardware/mechanical level—that is, with wires and voltages instead of with programs and codes. The disadvantage of this kind of handshaking is that it can be used only where devices can be physically connected through a cable. This makes it unsuitable for use with modems. This is illustrated schematically in Figure 2.6.

This diagram points up an important distinction between the kinds of signals of the interface: *data* signals and *control* signals. For our purposes, data signals are simply the pins which actually transmit and receive the characters, while control signals are everything else.

To Figure 2.6, let's add a concrete example of handshaking to illustrate the concept. Suppose that your modem is the kind that can automatically answer the telephone. Further assume that it is connected to your home telephone line. If your friends call while your modem is turned on, they are greeted by the obnoxious tones that modems produce. You need a way to prevent your modem from answering the

The character inserted by the computer is usually the ASCII character END OF TEXT (number 3, control-D), or ETX. When the receiving device is ready for another chunk of data, the character it sends back to the computer is the ASCII character ACKNOWLEDGE (number 6, control-F), or ACK. This form of software handshaking is therefore known as the ETX/ ACK protocol.

telephone unless you are at your computer and ready to handle the call. Your modem must monitor the computer's condition and respond accordingly. This is handshaking. Let's see how this can be done by looking at Figure 2.7.

In this example, when the terminal's power switch is turned off, the voltage at pin 20 is 0 volts. This 0 voltage is carried by the interface cable to the modem's pin 20. It is fairly standard that a modem will do absolutely nothing until it detects a positive voltage greater than 3 volts at its pin 20. In this manner—by virtue of the 0 volts at pin 20— the modem in our example is restrained from all action. Now, the terminal is internally wired so that just switching it on automatically causes a large voltage (say, 12 volts) to appear at its pin 20. This voltage is conducted through the cable to the modem's pin 20. When the

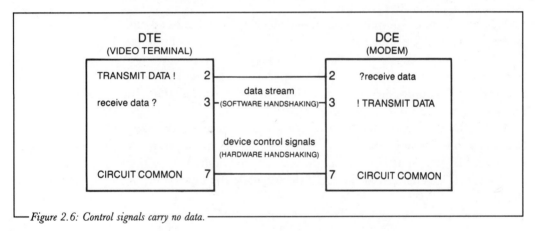

Figure 2.6: Control signals carry no data.

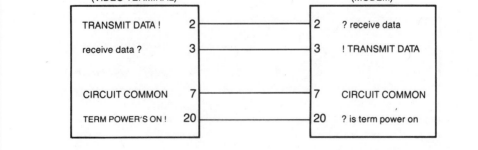

Figure 2.7: Modem won't answer unless terminal power is on.

modem's interface detects this voltage, its circuitry is activated, permitting it to function normally.

Notice that when seen from the perspective of the DTE device, pin 20 is an **output** (i.e., generates signals), but when seen from the perspective of the DCE is an **input** (i.e., detects signals). This is an extension of the "point of view" concept we developed previously about transmitted and received data. To avoid confusion, pins and signals are, by convention, named and discussed from the point of view of the DTE device. This means that unless explicitly stated otherwise, any mention of **TRANSMITTED DATA** will refer to the signal on pin 2; conversely, pin 2 will by default be assumed to carry **TRANSMITTED DATA.** Our schematic representation of outputs and inputs as ! and ?, together with the upper/lowercase notation is intended to help keep this matter of perspective straight.

This basic action—output to input—is all there is to handshaking. There are generally two or three such input/output pairs on an interface that allow one device to "talk" to the other. Nor is the conversation between devices limited to one direction. Using the same handshaking scheme, we could also inform the terminal that the modem is powered up as shown in Figure 2.8.

This additional handshake between the pin 6's is functionally identical to the one between the pin 20's: the assertion of an output pin is recognized by the input of the other device. The only difference is that the output (!) is generated at the DCE device while the input (?) is on the DTE.

The power-up handshaking between modem and terminal as we

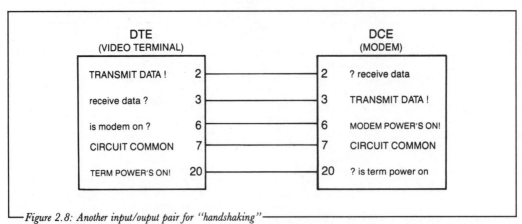

Figure 2.8: Another input/ouput pair for "handshaking"

have developed it so far happens to be the kind of interfacing described in the RS-232-C standard. As we have repeatedly observed, however, there is in practice no guarantee that your modem and/or terminal will implement any or all of these handshaking features. The manufacturer of your equipment may arbitrarily decide to apply some of the standard handshaking, no handshaking at all, or to invent a scheme of his own.

Even though microcomputer interface conventions may otherwise bear little resemblance to the official RS-232-C standard, the names given in the standard for data and handshaking signals are conventional and occur in all literature on the subject. Let's now apply these common names to our illustration. Remember, a "data set" is just another name for a modem.

In addition to their official names, each signal has an unofficial abbreviation, as shown below.

TRANSMITTED DATA   = TxD (also TD)
RECEIVED DATA   = RxD (also RD)
DATA TERMINAL READY = DTR
DATA SET READY   = DSR

In Figure 2.9 we see how our interface looks with official names installed. Notice that the names given to the inputs and outputs are the same for *both* devices.

A significant change has occurred to the diagram in Figure 2.9. Have you spotted it? The names of the signal *and* their pin numbers are *exactly* the same for DCE and DTE. They are, however, functionally

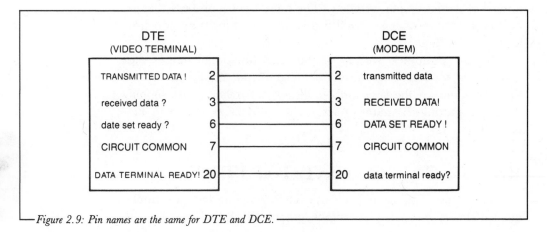

Figure 2.9: Pin names are the same for DTE and DCE.

exactly opposite—an output on the DTE is an input on the DCE (and vice versa), but the name or the pin number doesn't change. Although in reality it *receives* data from the DTE, the modem's pin 2 is officially named **TRANSMITTED DATA;** the only thing that identifies it as an input is our use of the **?**.

This point cannot be repeated too frequently, so think about the relationships, turn them over in your mind. Many find this dual role of pins and names to be perplexing. In fact, misunderstanding of this relationship is responsible for much of the confusion concerning the RS-232-C interface. It is helpful to realize that since the interface standard concerns interfacing DTEs to DCEs, an ordinary cable will make all necessary input/output and output/input connections. Still, the existence of pins with identical numbers and identical names but with inverse functions can cause considerable befuddlement.

As long as you're interfacing complementary devices, it all seems *soooo* simple. But (without dwelling upon the matter now) briefly consider the connections made between two devices of the same "sex." Suppose the serial port on your computer is configured DCE (will transmit on pin 2), but you want to connect a modem, which is also configured as a DCE. Now both devices are trying to transmit on the same wire, receive on the same wire, and their power-up handshaking is backwards.

Add to this situation a few eccentric conventions and you find yourself doing the "232 Tango," danced to the strains of "Anything Goes." It is for this purpose—the nonstandard interfacing of devices of the same sex—that you must try to think in terms of function instead of names or pin numbers. The names and numbers change, but the functions do not. We'll return to this point time and time again for clarification.

In earlier examples, we placed the pins' functional names—for example, Is Modem On?—inside the diagrams for the devices. Now, since the names are the same for both devices, we might as well simplify things by putting the names back *between* devices as shown in Figure 2.10.

RS-232-C "COMPATIBILITY"

While some of the signals on the RS-232-C interface are implemented almost universally on micros, others are applied liberally with out regard to any established practice. Before proceeding, it will be helpful to summarize exactly what can be expected from any device claiming to be "RS-232-C compatible."

Areas of RS-232-C Compatibility

The prescribed electrical characteristics (voltages, etc.) of the interface are, by necessity, closely observed. If a device claims to be "RS-232-C compatible" it means that you can connect it to another such "compatible" device without damaging or blowing up either. This guarantees that they will match well enough electrically to permit the exchange of data.

The voltage levels assigned for zero and one will correspond to those described in the standard. The voltage/logic definitions are different for data signals and control signals, so the use of 0 and 1 can actually cause misunderstandings. This difference will be discussed in detail in Chapter 5, but in the meantime, you are cautioned to postpone the natural tendency to think in terms of logic levels. To avoid any uncertainty about the matter of logic, we will always refer to control inputs as being either *enabled* (that is, turned on), or *disabled* (turned off). Control outputs are *asserted* when activated and *inhibited* when deactivated.

The plugs will probably fit the jacks. These terms—plug and jack—seem to be a source of eternal confusion. Connectors with pins are male, those with holes are female. A convenient mnemonic device is the paradox, "jack is female." The existence of pins or holes determines the sex of a connector, *not* which connector's outer sleeve fits inside

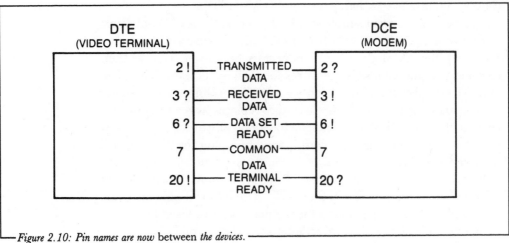

Figure 2.10: Pin names are now between the devices.

the other's. Pins are always manufactured in a recessed connector to protect the user from any hazardous voltages that might be present. For example, the DB-25 female connector (the one with holes) fits *inside* the male connector. We avoid this semantical difficulty by using the name *receptacle* instead of "jack."

Even though the pin assignments are dictated in the standard, the connectors themselves are not. The D-shaped DB-25 connector, however, has become an *ad hoc* standard. It is theoretically possible for a manufacturer to use a nonstandard or even a custom-made connector, yet still claim RS-232-C compatibility. The Otrona Attache computer, for example, uses a connector with only 15 pins, yet is advertised as being compatible with the RS-232-C interface standard. Strictly speaking, the connector must be able to pass all 21 signals described in the manual *and* have them correctly assigned in order to be truly compatible. In these instances, however, the use of a unique connector is far more noteworthy (and irksome) than the omission of irrelevant pins.

To use the standard's hazy language, the receptacle is "associated" with the DCE and the male connector with the DTE. This is interpreted to mean that DTEs should use a female connector and DCEs a male. Because it allows easy identification of a device as DCE or DTE, this association is potentially very valuable. More important, the presence of two identical connectors clearly announces that an interface will not function without special treatment. It is, alas, seldom observed. The female connector is usually installed for both DTE and DCE. When you *do* find a piece of equipment with a male connector mounted on the chassis, you can be reasonably certain that it is a DTE.

This refusal to accept simple standards such as the sex of connectors is annoying to everyone who has to deal with interfacing. Manufacturers say they do not use male connectors because it requires their customers to purchase separate cables for each application. This is an odd defense: the public has been successfully dealing with a similar phenomenon for years as 3-wire hardware replaces twin wiring in electrical outlets. Imagine your indignation upon discovering your new toaster had a receptacle on its cord instead of a plug, or that you had to rewire your new television set because its manufacturer and the electrician who wired your home did not have similar notions about customer convenience. The extra couple of cents spent on connectors is insignificant in comparison to the mental anguish caused by having to ascertain the electrical sex of an interface experimentally.

NO COMMENT DEPARTMENT

For some reason, IBM chose to put a DB-25 connector with male pins on the asynchronous board. This is directly contrary to the more common practice that puts the male pins on the cable and the female sockets on the chassis.

This means that when you approach the IBM PC with your trusty RS-232-C cable that you have used a 100 (sic) times before, it won't fit! You can make a female to female adaptor, but why should you have to?
—InfoWorld Report Card, September 1, 1983

It is interesting to note how the historical character of the printing terminal affects us today. Because of the speed limitations of a printing terminal, the sheer volume of paper to reckon with, and the noise produced, programmers tried to keep computer responses to a minimum. This historical tendency toward taciturnity and brevity persists today—except that we say that such programs are not "user-friendly."

A few pins on the connector are absolutely predictable:

pin 2 ⟩—transmitted / received data
pin 3 ⟋

pin 7   Circuit COMMON

If you discover a device that does not implement these signals on these pins, forget about any guidance from the interface standard.

Your terminal will probably be a DTE. When the standards were written, terminals were usually printing terminals; there were no video displays like those in use today. Instead, the computer responded to all commands by printing them. Printer interfaces therefore are traditionally configured DTE.

Microcomputer manufacturers have no way to predict whether customers will connect their computers to DTE or DCE devices. Thus, when they decide if their serial interfaces are to be configured DCE or DTE, they are making a decision that will prove wrong half the time. Because of this ambiguity, it is becoming common for computers with two serial ports to label one "printer" (with DCE pin assignments) and the other "communication/modem" (with DTE assignments).

Your modem will probably be a DCE. Because the RS-232-C standard was intended to standardize this interface, modems are nearly always DCE; however, a few modem manufacturers—mindful that computer manufacturers can't decide if their serial ports should be DTE or DCE—have begun to include switches inside their equipment to permit the user to rearrange the traditional DCE pin assignments to DTE. Thus, even the holy distinction that a modem is, by definition, Data Communications Equipment, is beginning to blur.

IN SUMMARY

Before proceeding, let's review the important points covered so far.

Data may be transferred byte-by-byte. This form of byte-oriented transmission is known as parallel. Although fast, it is acutely sensitive to its electrical environment. In addition, its expense, coupled with the physical bulk of the wires themselves, make it undesirable for long distances.

Data may be transferred bit-by-bit. This is known as serial transmission. It is transferred at much slower speeds than parallel, but this makes it much less susceptible (though not immune) to any prevailing environmental conditions. Since it can be transferred using as few as two wires, it is more economical for long distances.

To allow safe interchange of information with the outside world, an interface is required. The most commonly used serial interface used on microcomputers is the EIA RS-232-C. Originally written to facilitate the interconnection of terminals (DTE or Data Terminal Equipment) and modems (DCE or Data Communication Equipment), the RS-232-C interface is awkward to use on other kinds of equipment.

Handshaking is the process by which one device monitors the status of another and responds accordingly.

The following points relate to the details of the RS-232-C interface.

- *Data* is exchanged between devices on pins 2 and 3.
- *Software handshaking* is accomplished by imbedding control characters in the data stream.
- *Hardware handshaking* is accomplished by means of wires shared between the two interfaces. Pins designated as outputs (!) are mated by cable with corresponding pins designated as inputs (?).
- Although the signal names and pin assignments for DTE and DCE devices may be identical, they have complementary functions.

In the next chapter, we'll take a functional look at the device that is most commonly used for serial data transfer—the UART. Although there are several brands and types of UARTs, they are more or less functionally equivalent. The functions of this device are important because they have almost single-handedly dictated the personality of the microcomputer serial interface as it exists today.

THE UART: ELVES IN THE BASEMENT

3

So far we have focused upon the preliminary concepts involved in serial data communications. We outlined the difference between DTE (**D**ata **T**erminal **E**quipment) and DCE (**D**ata **C**ommunication **E**quipment). We treated certain pins on the RS-232-C interface connector as conceptual units for passing back and forth various data and control signals. We assigned the official names and pin numbers, and got a feeling for the notion that one device can control another through handshaking.

A conceptual level of understanding is an indispensable learning tool, but, because of its very theoretical nature, doesn't stand up to real tasks. Trying to solve knotty, workaday problems with only a conceptual understanding is like throwing baseballs at fuzzy cats at a carnival. In addition to our conceptual understanding, we need to develop the *why* and *how*. We need, for example, to understand what actually happens when **DATA TERMINAL READY** is asserted, or **DATA SET READY** is enabled, or *how* the dual role of single-pin input/output is really achieved. In short, we need to render these concepts into reality. To this end, we'll peer behind the connector to examine the devices that actually perform the serial I/O.

It should not surprise you to learn that the connectors and cables themselves are entirely passive and perform no transmission or reception of data. Clearly, other devices must be at work behind the connector. These devices are called *Universal Asynchronous Receiver/Transmitters*, or UARTs for short. In order to understand the process of data transfer clearly, we'll temporarily suspend our discussion of the interface itself while we look at these important devices. As always, our approach will be functional—only an intuitive knowledge of electronics or circuitry is required. We'll then return to the subject of the RS-232-C interface with a more complete understanding of events and their causes.

Processor I/O

Microcomputer users are lucky. Virtually the entire process of serial I/O is performed by the single kind of integrated circuit, known generically as a UART. Before UARTs were developed, the process of I/O, down to its most fundamental level, was controlled directly by the computer's microprocessor itself. A program was therefore responsible for even the most minute details required to convert parallel to serial data, then send the bits one at a time to the correct pin on the interface at precisely the correct time. Because such bit-oriented programs veritably gulp processor time and computer resources, they tend to be expensive and tedious to write. I/O was, understandably, kept to an absolute minimum because programmers didn't like to code it and customers didn't like to pay for it.

Because it relieves the processor of the burdensome minutiae of serial I/O, the UART is known as a *service device*. In contrast to processor-controlled I/O, a program "driving" a UART doesn't grapple with details. The programmer treats the UART as a mailbox into which outbound characters are dropped for dispatch, or from which inbound characters are fetched. For all the processor or programmer knows, the serial/parallel conversion, the timing, and the associated logic are being done in the basement by elves.

It is not difficult to understand why this blister-packed technology came quickly to dominate the micro scene. Since micros contained limited memory and operated at slower speeds than larger computers, the UART became popular because it conserves these valuable resources by obviating processor-intensive programming. Although a few early microcomputers performed processor I/O (for example, Morrow's "Keyed-Up 8080" or "Speak-Easy I/O" boards from the early 1970s), it is today difficult to locate examples of this technology even as conversation pieces. In fact, so thoroughly has the UART permeated the thinking about serial I/O, that programs that perform processor I/O are now referred to as "software" UARTs.

It is tempting to infer that UARTs are somehow inextricably associated with the RS-232-C interface. Not so. UARTs are used in myriad serial applications besides those involving the RS-232-C interface. The opposite association, however, is valid: wherever you find a DB-25 connector on a microcomputer, you can almost bet that there's a UART behind it.

Dozens of models of UARTs are available. It is beyond the scope of this book to compare and contrast them. Instead, we will slowly build a functional model of a generic UART, explaining each section and how it interacts with the RS-232-C interface. As in the previous chapter, the format or the contents of the data itself is irrelevant to our purpose.

UART Fundamentals

Functionally, the UART—as its full name suggests—comprises a TRANSMITTER section for converting an 8-bit byte into a serial stream of eight bits and a RECEIVER section that reconverts an incoming stream of bits to a byte of data. In addition, there is a CONTROL AND STATUS section that, among other things, monitors the logic state of several input pins and, *when called upon by a program*, changes the logic level of several output pins. We previously made the analogy between serial I/O and leading a chain of elephants across a drawbridge. The CONTROL/STATUS section of the UART— shown in the center of Figure 3.2—is the *instrument panel* used by the programmer to lower the drawbridge.

Figure 3.1 illustrates these three sections. The top of the diagram

Figure 3.2: Making the data flow

shows the TRANSMITTER section. Here parallel data from the right arrives at the transmitter from the data lines (known as the data bus). Serial bit data is output at the left.

The bottom of the diagram shows the RECEIVER section. Notice that incoming bits arrive at the receiver from the left, are converted to parallel data, then are sent to the data lines at the right.

It is important to observe that both the RECEIVER and TRANSMITTER sections share the same data lines. Whenever a character is to be transmitted, the TRANSMITTER section is connected to the data lines to fetch the character. Conversely, when a character has been received and reassembled into a byte, the RECEIVER is connected to the data lines while the byte is transferred. Through "steering" commands in the software, the CONTROL/STATUS section

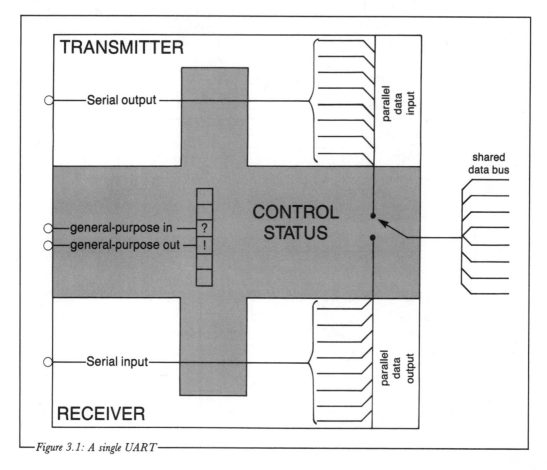

Figure 3.1: A single UART

automatically determines whether the data lines should be connected to the transmitter or to the receiver. This switching action is symbolized in our diagram by an arrow on the bit/line: ⟶

Input and Output Logic

In addition to arbitrating which section is attached to the data bus, the CONTROL/STATUS section also presides over the logic state of several general-purpose input and output pins. These are represented in Figure 3.2 by the row of boxes (some empty, for now) containing our input (?) and output (!) notation. Each of these boxes represents one of the "instruments" on the panel. For example, by checking the contents of these boxes, the program is able to ascertain whether the logic status of pin GENERAL PURPOSE INPUT #1 is at logic level zero or one. On the other hand, the programmer can *change* the logic level on pin GENERAL PURPOSE OUTPUT #1.

THE UART
AND THE RS-232-C INTERFACE

The process of reading the logic status of the inputs and changing the logic status of outputs is the mechanism by which the UART interacts with the RS-232-C interface. Before we recall the diagram of the RS-232-C interface as we left it last chapter in Figure 3.3, it should be pointed out that not all serial peripheral devices contain actual UART

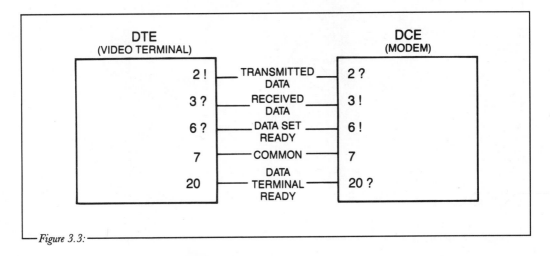

Figure 3.3:

chips. This is unimportant, however, because we are concerned with a generic UART. Regardless of how an interface is constructed, if it behaves as if it were a UART, it *is*, for our purpose, a UART.

Figure 3.4 should be worth 1K words in demonstrating how a UART connects with the RS-232-C interface.

The **TRANSMITTED DATA** (pin 2) of the DTE is nothing but the serial data output of the UART's TRANSMITTER SECTION. The **TRANSMITTED DATA** (pin 2) input of the DCE is (surprise, surprise!) connected to the UART's RECEIVER SECTION.

The **DATA TERMINAL READY** (pin 20) output of the DTE device is simply one of the general-purpose UART outputs, while **DATA TERMINAL READY** (pin 20) input of the DCE device is connected to its UART's general-purpose input.

It is significant that **DATA TERMINAL READY** and **DATA SET READY**, names so formidable to the ear, turn out to be mere "general-purpose" inputs and outputs. They are called "general-purpose" because their behavior has no *automatic* effect on the behavior of the UART. General purpose inputs should be thought of as indicator lights on the control panel: they monitor the logic level of the input, but exert no *inherent* influence on the UART's behavior. Likewise, although its logic status is continuously reported on the instrument panel, a general–purpose output changes only when commanded by software.

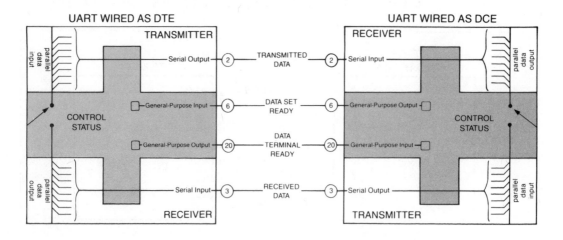

————*Figure 3.4: Our mythical interface from Chapter 2*————————————

THE UART
AND PROGRAM CONTROL

The question now arises, "If nothing happens when these lines are manipulated, how did our power-up handshaking take place? How did the computer know how to respond to an enabled **dsr** lead?" The answer is at once obvious and profound. The computer responded because a program was monitoring the status of the input connected to the interface's **DATA SET READY** pin. When this change was detected, the program proceeded upon its way. When thinking at such a basic nuts-and-bolts level, it is easy to forget that all intelligent action by a computer ultimately is the result of software. There is absolutely nothing built into the hardware that dictates that a change in the general-purpose input (here *arbitrarily* assigned the title **DATA SET READY** on the DTE) *must* result in a specific action. The program might, for example, just as easily (but not so likely) have interpreted the enabling of the general-purpose input to mean that the entire system should be rebooted. Chapter 12 illustrates how a UART in concert with software is able to alter the RS-232-C interface.

UARTs—or anything else this basic—are not preprogrammed to conform to the logic control dictated by the RS-232-C interface standard. The functions of these general purpose inputs and outputs are left entirely to the programmer's discretion. Indeed, the great diversity among "RS-232-C compatible" devices reflects this freedom. Sometimes the programmer might be conservative, disinclined to throw past interfacing conventions to the winds. Or the programmer might be a young Turk—brilliant, but unschooled in RS-232-C interface standard orthodoxy—whose attitude is "DATA SET WHO?"

HANDSHAKING REVISITED

Literalists would fairly argue that our previous discussion of handshaking was not about handshaking at all, but about *control logic,* also known as *protocol:* signals to guarantee that a finite number of events can occur only in an orderly, predetermined sequence. In this large context, the exchange of data is just *one* of the possible events that may be under control. By contrast, handshaking, as we defined it in Chapter 2, involves the *control and regulation* of the *flow* of *data* across the interface. This distinction, while perhaps a touch pedantic, is nevertheless a good reminder that our avowed task in this book is to explore how *data* is transported between two points.

When we began the topic of handshaking in Chapter 2, we saw that the data flow between devices could be controlled either by software or by hardware. In this chapter, we'll continue to focus on the hardware method, but first we need to discuss why handshaking of any kind is required in the first place. To this end, we now return to the problem of interfacing our mythical printer.

The Print Buffer

As serial data is transmitted across the RS-232-C interface, it can be visualized as a string of characters moving between devices (like our chain of elephants), one bit slowly following the one before it. A computer can usually transmit characters much faster than the receiving peripheral device can process them. In the case of a printer, characters arrive much faster than they can be printed. Incoming characters, therefore, must be stashed somewhere in the order of their arrival until their turn comes to be printed. The place where the characters are held—the *print buffer*—usually consists of only a few hundred bytes of memory in the printer itself.

Print Buffer Overflow

Since characters are being put into the print buffer much faster than they are being taken out for printing, sooner or later there will be no more space for incoming characters. When the print buffer is full, attempts to add a new character will result in its irretrievable loss.

In communications, the word protocol *is a fuzzword. It disguises its meaning to blend with the sentence in which it is used. In most usage, it's a smokescreen for fuzzy thought or inadequate learning. Even in context, it often doesn't have an unambiguous meaning. When knowledgeable people do use it, they generally intend it to mean what we are here calling device control logic. When used loosely, it usually means "prior agreement." If it doesn't make sense in that context, just ignore it altogether: a word ignored is better than one misunderstood.*

Here are three such usages, taken from respected microcomputer books and journals:

1. ". . . printer recognizes all the standard ASCII protocols." There is no such thing as an ASCII protocol.

Figure 3.5

2. "Baud and parity are but two of the protocols that confuse the novice." No wonder he's confused. These aren't protocols. Baud is a unit of measure for the speed of serial transmission. Parity is a basic method of error checking.
3. Here's the name of a chapter in a book on data communications: RS-232-C and Other Physical-Layer Protocols.

This condition—known as buffer overflow—is reminiscent of a certain type of problem used in high school math books. One such problem assumes that you are filling a water container faster than you are draining it. "How long before the container overflows?" or "What will the capacity be after two hours?" are typical questions asked.

The printer logic answers questions such as these every time a new character arrives or whenever one is printed. The printer in this way calculates if its buffer is nearing its maximum capacity. When the buffer is about 90 percent *full*, the printer logic starts calling for a halt in characters. The flow of characters is temporarily suspended. Then, when printing reduces buffer to within 10 percent of empty, the printer logic sends out a request for more characters. In this way the printer exercises control over the flow of incoming data.

Signaling a Full Buffer

This calls for classic handshaking. Recall that a printer may signal "buffer overflow" either by sending special *control* characters back to the computer, or by changing the logic state of a pin on the RS-232-C interface. In either case, the printer requests the computer to halt transmission of characters until a subsequent signal communicates that the print buffer can once again accept more characters.

Figure 3.6

The RS-232-C interface standard defines an input/output pair that closely approximates the signaling just described: **CLEAR TO SEND** (**CTS**) and **REQUEST TO SEND** (**RTS**). These are added to our printer-computer interface in Figure 3.7.

If you have just settled into intellectual comfort with the concept of input/output pairs with the matching names and pin numbers, beware of these. You have likely been disciplining yourself to interpret names from the point of view of the DTE device. That is, indeed, the correct procedure. But look at these two names: from its name—REQUEST TO SEND—one would naturally expect this signal to be an input. Wrong. It is a DTE output whose purpose is to *assert* a **REQUEST TO SEND** (**RTS**). Since it's an output, DEMAND would have been a more descriptive name. Similarly, you would suppose that **CLEAR TO SEND** would be an output, but instead it's a DTE input for enabling transmission. The best way to understand this is by expanding our UART diagram with a bit more detail as shown in Figure 3.8.

The whole object of this handshake is, of course, to disable the transmitter of the computer's UART. Look closely at the way SPECIAL-PURPOSE INPUT #1 is drawn. Like all the other inputs and outputs, it extends to its box to indicate that it's a part of the CONTROL/STATUS section. From there, however, the box is

Previously we discussed the ETX/ACK (End-Of-Text/Acknowledge) software handshaking protocol, where the transmitter was in control of the handshake.

A much more common kind of software handshaking protocol occurs when the receiver controls the handshake. The printer accepts characters until its buffer is full, at which time it initiates the handshake by sending a "turn off" character—usually the ASCII character DC3 (number 19, or control-S)—back to the computer. When the computer receives this character, it goes on hold. When the print buffer is ready for

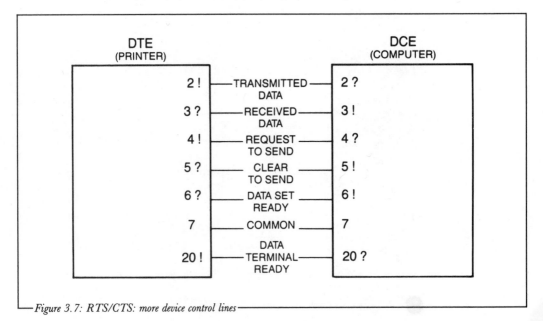

Figure 3.7: RTS/CTS: more device control lines

another load of characters, the printer sends a "turn on" character— usually the ASCII character DC1 (number 17, or control-Q)—to the computer. Upon receipt of this character, the computer resumes sending characters where it left off. Since there is some variation in the control characters used, the generic name for this receiver-driven, software handshake is X-ON/ X-OFF.

connected by a dotted line to the **TRANSMITTED DATA** line, part of which extends through the CONTROL/STATUS section. The dotted line ends at our symbol for a switch: ⎯⎯⎯▶

Pausing The Transmitter: Special-Purpose Input #1

The transmitter line's passage through the STATUS/CONTROL section is one of the keys to understanding how handshaking is performed. This switch is a diagrammatic representation of a simple, but very important process: when SPECIAL-PURPOSE INPUT #1 is enabled, the transmitter operates normally; when it is disabled, the transmitter is interrupted and will not send data.

The accompanying GENERAL-PURPOSE OUTPUT #2 is just like the other general-purpose output—its logic status is reported on the control panel, and can be changed, but it has no *inherent* effect on the UART's operations.

Like all inputs and outputs, the logic status of the SPECIAL-PURPOSE INPUT #1 is reported on the instrument panel. It is considered to be special-purpose because its logic level *does* affect the operation of the UART—it switches the TRANSMITTER section on *and* off!

Let's now look at Figure 3.9, a diagram of the UARTs connected through the RS-232-C interface.

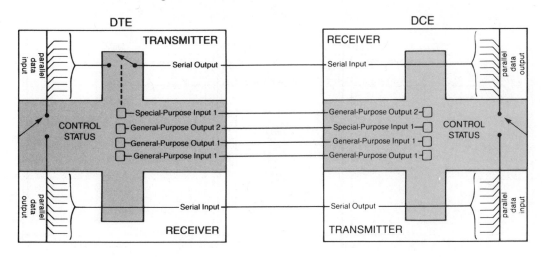

⎯Figure 3.8: Disabling the transmitter⎯

This appears to be exactly the connection we need in order for our printer to handshake with our computer. When the printer's buffer approaches maximum capacity, the printer inhibits its **RTS** output. This disables the computer UART's SPECIAL-PURPOSE INPUT #1 which, in turn, shuts off the computer's transmitter. Voila! The computer pauses in transmission until its SPECIAL-PURPOSE INPUT #1 is again asserted.

The name actually assigned to pin 8 by the EIA document is **RECEIVED LINE SIGNAL DETECT,** *not a name that dances lightly from the tongue. Even though many modems do not employ a true carrier (see Chapter 12), the name* **DCD** *is in such general use that we (reluctantly) use it here.*

Pausing The Receiver: Special-Purpose Input #2

We need only one additional function to have a general picture of a micro's RS-232-C interface. We have seen how a UART's transmitter can be interrupted by disabling its SPECIAL-PURPOSE INPUT #1. In exactly the same way, some UARTs employ a SPECIAL-PURPOSE INPUT #2 to disable their receivers. This function is denoted diagramatically in Figure 3.10 by a dotted line between the input and the switch symbol located in the receiver line itself.

This input interacts with the UART in exactly the same way as the other special-purpose input except that here it controls the UART's receiver. When this input is enabled, the receiver is permitted to reconvert incoming serial data to bytes. When the input is disabled, however, the receiver ignores incoming data and no conversion takes

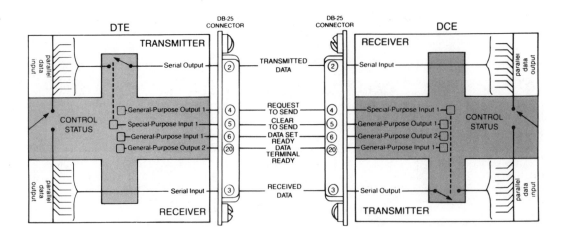

—*Figure 3.9: Completed model with DB-25's*—

place. For reasons explained in the chapter on modems, the SPECIAL-PURPOSE INPUT #2 is generally associated with pin 8 on RS-232-C interface, **DATA CARRIER DETECT** (**DCD**).

In Figure 3.11, you see the completed functional diagram of the

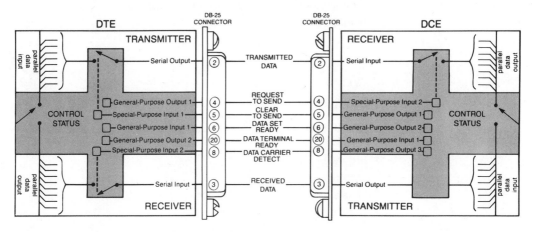

Figure 3.10: Disabling the receiver

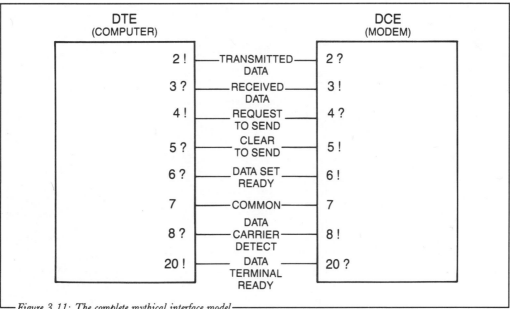

Figure 3.11: The complete mythical interface model

RS-232-C interface as we have developed it. As an aid to understanding, you should try to visualize the diagram complete with the generic UART connections.

You will be delighted to learn that there are no more pins, functions, or signals to learn. The rest of this book will deal with the manipulation of these eight leads.

4

TRICKS AND FLIPS: COPING WITH THE REAL WORLD

MURKY WATERS

Although it should not be given undue emphasis, we note that we've now moved into uncharted areas with the RS-232-C interface standard. Until now, we have been able to stay approximately within the boundaries of the RS-232-C interface standard, but the hand-shaking between a computer and a printer causes our first real departure from it. Remember, it was never intended for this kind of handshaking.

The purpose of this chapter, then, is to explore specifically how the the standard RS-232-C interface fails us in common microcomputer interfacing situations. From this understanding we can go on to learn how manufacturers have "tricked" the interface into working where it isn't supposed to.

In order to understand the implications of interfacing a printer to a computer, let's see how **REQUEST TO SEND** and **CLEAR TO SEND** were intended to work. Consider the interface in Figure 4.1.

Notice that in this diagram, the computer is a DCE and the printer is a DTE.

REQUEST TO SEND is the way a DTE informs a DCE that it wishes to transmit data. When the DCE's **rts** input is enabled, and if it is available to accept data, it replies by asserting its **CLEAR TO SEND**. When the DTE sees this reply—its **cts** input is enabled—it begins to transmit. Thus, **RTS/CTS** is a hardware protocol preceding transmission *from* a DTE *to* a DCE.

This sounds simple, doesn't it? It is, but this is not *exactly* what we need to do to interface the printer to the computer. With our mythical printer and computer, the sole direction of data flow is in the *opposite* direction, from computer to printer, or DCE to DTE. But our DTE printer doesn't transmit data! Therefore, at no time, does the printer (a DTE) need to use **RTS** for querying the DCE computer about its status.

In order to conform to the RS-232-C interface standard, our interface requires a pair of input/output signals by which the DCE can request and receive permission to send data to the DTE. The method we have just devised—where the printer signals the computer—may, at first sight, appear to be just such a mechanism. But not quite: our DTE is not granting the DCE permission to transmit, so much as it is forcibly restraining it from transmitting.

As you might have guessed by now, the function we need is not a part of the RS-232-C interface standard. This means that there is no "official" process by which a DTE printer can be queried to ascertain if it is prepared to accept data. This leads to a startling conclusion: a DTE must *always* be ready to accept data. Unfortunately, printers, by their very nature, *cannot* be ready to accept data at all times.

This illustrates how the RS-232-C interface standard breaks down when it's used outside the purview of the modem/terminal interface.

BABES IN THE WOODS DEPARTMENT

. . . the solution is to check the handshaking signals between the computer and printer. For a serial port, the signals are Request-to-Send (RTS) and Clear-to-Send (CTS) . . .
—BYTE, *June, 1983*

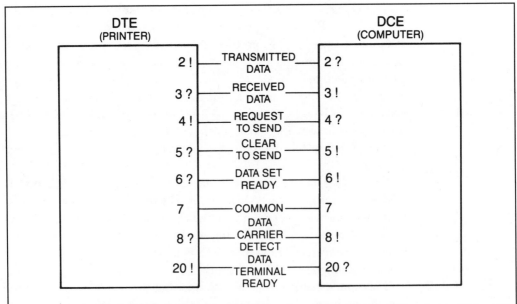

Figure 4.1: *A mythical printer/computer interface*

There is actually some official support for assigning handshaking to an unassigned pin. Section four of the standard contains this marvelous sentence: "Additional interchange circuits [read signals] not defined herein . . . may be provided by mutual agreement."

The mere fact that a printer is DTE and the computer is DCE forces a departure from normal RS-232-C interfacing techniques. So, in order to make most printers work, manufacturers are forced to improvise. Once they have realized that it *is not possible to conform to the standard when interfacing a printer,* some compromising decisions must be made. The first is to designate the pin that will be responsible for handshaking. Well, **RTS** *does* sound reasonable, doesn't it? Or how about **DTR**, since the printer is actually not *ready* for characters? An even better idea: avoid compatibility problems altogether by assigning the handshaking signal to a pin whose function is not even defined in the RS-232-C.

Once the necessity of deviation has been conceded, the question of degree becomes moot, and other modifications suddenly seem sensible. For instance, unless software handshaking is being used (requiring the printer to send control characters back to the DCE), the **RECEIVED DATA** line can be eliminated. Or if handshaking is assigned to, say, **DRT** pin 20, **CLEAR TO SEND** is expendable.

These are precisely the kind of issues that are encountered everytime an RS-232-C device is designed, and almost every manufacturer deals with them differently. Interfacing RS-232-C microcomputer components is largely a matter of deciphering each manufacturer's peculiar improvisations. Some manufacturers try to make their equipment *truly* "RS-232-C compatible," while others provide only a minimum application of signals. The important point to keep in mind is that in order to use the RS-232-C interface, an engineering decision must be made about how to torture the standard interface. The remainder of this book is devoted to explaining the most common decisions.

TRICKING THE INTERFACE

The pins and signals vary widely among interfaces. One manufacturer may decide to include the **DTR/drt** control signals, another **RTS/cts**. Accordingly, you eventually encounter a situation where an input on one side of the interface does not receive the complementary output from the other side of the interface. Our printer, for example, doesn't work at all unless its **dsr** input is enabled. But what if the computer to which we connect it does not supply the signal needed to enable it?

In cases like these, we must *trick* the interface into thinking that the signals it expects are really there. It is not uncommon, for example, to find DTE devices that assert **DTR**, but *not* **RTS**. If such a device is connected to a DCE that requires its **rts** input to be enabled, the control logic can't be satisfied by an ordinary, straight-through cable as illustrated in Figure 4.2.

Suppose this DCE will not work unless its **rts** input is enabled, yet the DTE does not enable its **RTS** output. How to proceed? The necessary signal is borrowed from the DCE's **dtr** input, now high via the DTE's assertion. More precisely, we *share* the voltage asserted by the DTE's **DATA TERMINAL READY** with the DCE's **REQUEST TO SEND (rts)** input as shown in Figure 4.3.

In this figure, the DCE's enabled **dtr** input is *jumpered* to the **REQUEST TO SEND (RTS)**. A jumper is just a wire connecting the two pins. How can we so casually "share" voltages between pins? It works just the same as the electrical outlets in your home—several appliances (inputs) can easily share one electrical outlet (output). The interface is very generous in this area: a single output can be used to enable more than 40 inputs!

A similar problem frequently arises with printers that require *receiver* handshaking on their pin 8, **DATA CARRIER DETECT (dcd)** inputs. Unless the **DCE** being interfaced is a modem, its **DCD** output may

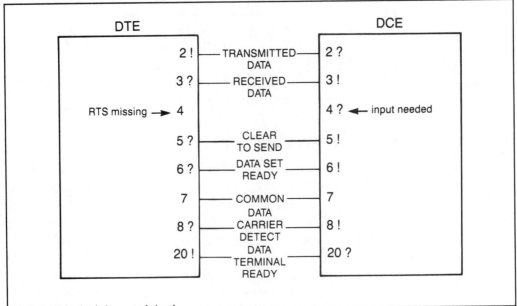

Figure 4.2: A missing control signal

never be asserted. As in the example above, the necessary signal must be brought over from another pin as shown in Figure 4.4.

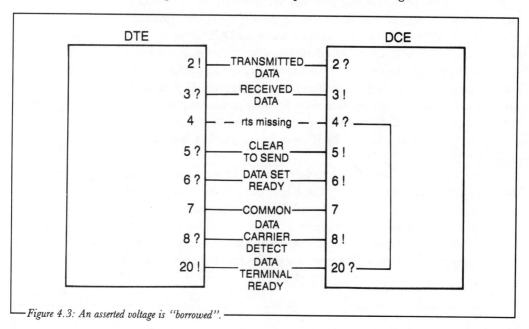

Figure 4.3: An asserted voltage is "borrowed".

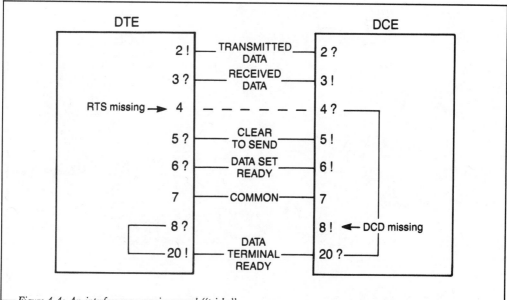

Figure 4.4: An interface may require several "tricks".

Interfacing Devices of The Same Sex

A special kind of interfacing problem arises when one attempts to interface two devices of the same sex. If purists complain when the standard RS-232-C interface is used to interface a DCE computer to a DTE printer (i.e., a device of complementary sex), the same-sex interface elicits screams of protest. This situation will arise about half the time, depending upon how the computer is configured. If your computer is DTE, you'll have to deal with it when connecting a printer. If your computer is DCE, you'll have to go through it with a modem. Count yourself among the lucky if your computer has one port of each sex.

To illustrate what a same-sex interface means, let's assume that our mythical computer is not a DCE, but a DTE as shown in Figure 4.6. This will produce some extremely anomalous connections.

Notice that outputs (!) are connected to outputs and inputs (?) to inputs. These connections provide no device control, no handshaking, and, of course, no data flow. We need a technique to restore the inputs and outputs to their "standard," complementary relationship. That is

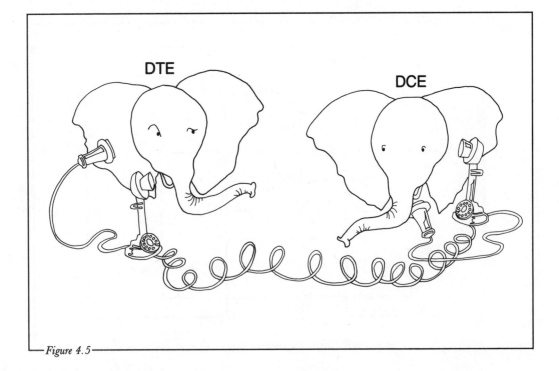

DTE   DCE

Figure 4.5

to say, we need to change the sex of *one* of the devices, the grandest trick of them all!

This can be accomplished in one of three ways.

1. Open either device, locate the wires of the RS-232-C interface, then swap the input/output pairs. Some equipment even provides internal switches to facilitate this procedure.

2. Construct a special cable with the pairs exchanged at one end.

3. Construct a custom connector.

We will discuss the relative merits of each of these methods in the case studies presented later. For now, you should focus on understanding *why* it is necessary to swap them. In Figure 4.8, this is shown diagramatically.

This procedure for restoring the correct input/output relationship is called "flipping," and a *flipped cable* or *flipped connector* cross-wires these pairs. By one method or another, inputs are patched to their complementary outputs and vice versa. Either side of the interface may be

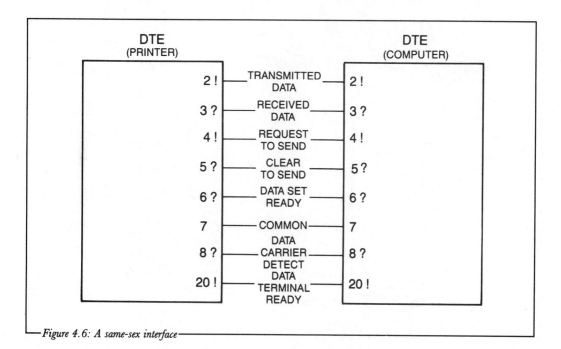

Figure 4.6: A same-sex interface

flipped: the printer could just as easily have been flipped to look like a DCE device.

But what can one do about the **dcd**'s on pin 8? It has no corresponding output with which to swap. How to deal with anomalies such as this is a practical interfacing problem which we'll cover in a later chapter. For the time being, ignore it or visualize them pulled up to **DTR**.

Figure 4.7: Changing the sex of one side only

LIFE IS HARSH
DEPARTMENT
The machine's owner
and I had problems
with printers during our
operation of the [IBM
PC XT] system, and it
took several weeks to get
them corrected. Numer-
ous calls—to the dealer,
to IBM's regional sales
office, to executives of
the franchise that had
sold my friend his PC
XT—ensued. We
finally uncovered the
problem and its solu-
tion, which is related to
the pin settings on our
serial-interface printers
and the need for special
cables.
—InfoWorld Report
Card, September 1,
1983

Installing tricks—flipping interfaces, jumpering the control signals and handshaking signals—is a routine part of RS-232-C interfacing. Unless both pieces of equipment were made by the same manufacturer, there is an excellent chance that you will have to puzzle out a jumpering configuration.

PIN FUNCTIONS

Here is a much-needed summary of the important pins on the RS-232-C interface. As always, these defintions are from the DTE's perspective.

PIN 1 **PROTECTIVE GROUND** This is unofficially called the "chassis ground." If a piece of equipment does not have a round prong on its AC plug, it should be connected through the pin 1's to one that does. This is to prevent electrical shock in the event of a power supply failure. This can be accomplished by using a cable that connects the device's pin 1's.

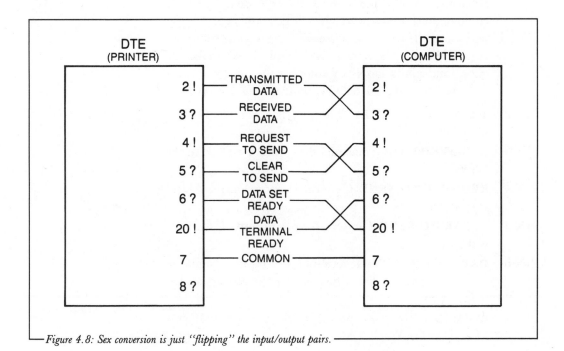

Figure 4.8: Sex conversion is just "flipping" the input/output pairs.

The function of this pin is frequently confused with that of pin 7, known as "common return." The center prong on the AC cord is *supposed* to lead eventually back to mother earth, hence the term "ground." In practice, however, this route can be rather circuitous, resulting in considerable resistance between the equipment and earth. When two pieces of equipment are connected to different power distribution feeders (in a very large building, for example), their paths to earth may be electrically different. The result is that their chassis are not electrically the same. This condition may actually disable communications, but can be effectively eliminated by joining the two chassis through the two pin 1's.

This situation doesn't arise very often. In fact, under ordinary circumstances, you are more likely to induce problems by connecting the pin 1's. A much more invidious kind of problem—called a *ground loop*—may result from unnecessarily connecting the chassis together through the cable. Ground loops make your equipment behave erratically, and seem to be dependent upon odd combinations of hardware, switch positions, etc. If your peripherals behave as if possessed, check your cables for connected pin 1's; you may be able to exorcize the ghosts and spirits simply by snipping the pin 1's.

In any case, in the RS-232-C standard, pin 1 is optional.

PIN 2   **TRANSMITTED DATA** Transmits data from the DTE to the DCE

PIN 3   **RECEIVED DATA** Transmits data from the DCE to the DTE

PIN 4   **REQUEST TO SEND** General-purpose output. Uses vary widely.

PIN 5   **CLEAR TO SEND** General-purpose input. Uses vary widely.

PIN 6   **DATA SET READY** General-purpose input to signal to the DTE that the DCE has been powered up and is ready to go.

PIN 7   **COMMON** Reference point for all interface voltages. MANDATORY.

PIN 8   **DATA CARRIER DETECT** Its uses vary, but on a DTE it's frequently used to disable data reception.

PIN 20   **DATA TERMINAL READY** General-purpose output. Generally used to signal to the DCE that the DTE has been powered up and is ready to go.

Many other pins are used on microcomputer interfaces, but most of the important activity occurs on these nine pins. The group—2,3,4,5,6,7,8,20—is called the BIG EIGHT. Where other pins are employed, they usually provide secondary or optional features unique to that manufacturer.

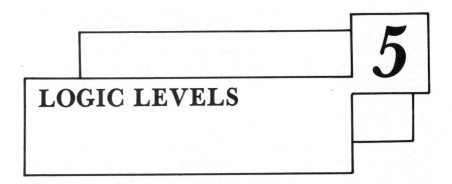

LOGIC LEVELS

We now come to examine the electrical definitions of the data. Notice that we are still not concerned with the *format* of the data, only the relationships between the logic levels and how they are represented by voltages.

This brief chapter is not intended as a perfunctory intellectual exercise. It contains explanations of many aspects of the interface which are not widely understood. It is fair to say that you can't really expect to interface RS-232-C compatible microcomputer equipment without a working knowledge of its logical characteristics. Moreover, familiarity with these ideas will make you more comfortable when you come to the actual case studies in Chapters 7 through 11.

For the sake of clarity, our drawings have all shown the UARTs connected directly to the DB-25 connector. In truth, this representation is incorrect. As a general rule, UARTs are operated from the same single 5 volt power supply as other integrated circuits inside the computer. The RS-232-C interface, however, defines its own unique electrical environment. Voltages ranging from +25 to −25 volts are possible under certain circumstances. Computer components frequently define logic levels in terms of the *magnitude* of a voltage; the standard, however, specifies *bipolar logic levels*. This means that the positivity and negativity of the voltage determines its logic level.

So between the UART and the connector itself must exist another physical layer of electronics to convert the UART's voltages to those specified by the RS-232-C interface standard. Typically, this conversion is accomplished with integrated circuits especially designed for RS-232-C interfacing. One type of IC, the *RS-232-C line driver*, translates the UART's output voltages to those required by the RS-232-C interface standard while another, the *RS-232-C line receiver*, converts the

RS-232-C voltages to the levels required by the UART circuitry. Figure 5.1 depicts this process of electrical translation.

Other than pointing out its importance in the general scheme of RS-232-C interfacing, we are absolutely uninterested in the details of the conversion process itself.

Logic Definitions

Data is transmitted "upside-down." In comparison to the logic conventions currently in use, the voltage/logic relationship on the interface is inverted: a positive voltage on the interface represents 0, while a negative voltage represents 1.

If we are to develop sound techniques for interfacing, we are obliged to understand the details of these relationships. Figure 5.2 illustrates the logical definitions for RS-232-C.

Note the inverted logic: 1 is assigned to the *negative* voltage levels, 0 to the positive. In order to guarantee 0, an output pin must assert a voltage between +5 and +15 volts. Similarly, a guaranteed 1 must lie between −5 and −15 volts. The "dead-band" between +5 and −5 is known as the *transition region* where logic levels are not defined. This means that any output between +5 and −5 volts might be ambiguously interpreted as *either* 0 or 1. Figure 5.3 illustrates the logical definitions for *inputs*.

The only difference between this definition and the one for *outputs* is the width of the transition region. An input's undefined logical zone

The Golden Eagle serial interface is considered to be DTE and follows all EIA standards. All signals are based on EIA RS-232-C levels. MARK = − 3v to − 27v, SPACE = + 3v to + 27v.
—Golden Eagle Manual

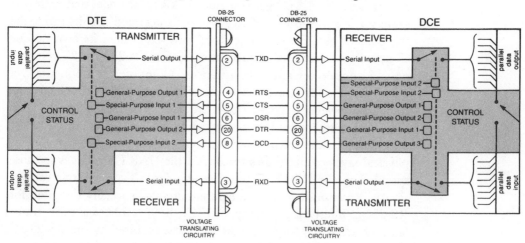

—*Figure 5.1: Another layer of electronics isolates the UART from the high RS-232-C voltages.*

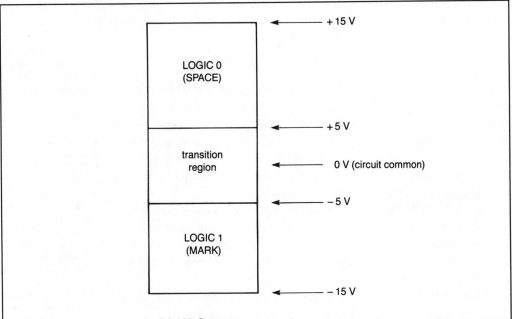

Figure 5.2: Logic definitions for RS-232-C outputs

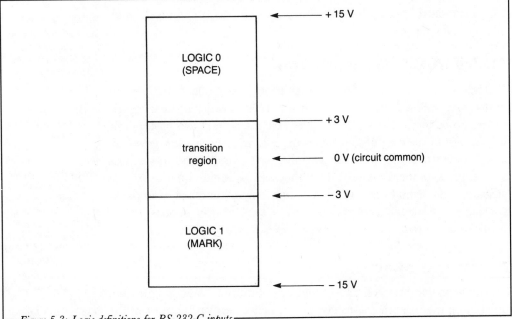

Figure 5.3: Logic definitions for RS-232-C inputs

is only six volts (from + 3 to − 3 volts), while the corresponding area for an output is 10 volts (from + 5 to − 5 volts). This apparently incidental difference is monumentally important.

Noise Margin

Officially, this difference between the definitions for the minimum permissible voltages is known as the circuit's *noise margin.* This means that some electrical noise is permitted along with the output voltage without adversely affecting the logic level at the input. This attribute is extremely valuable where cables must be run near devices that generate electrical interference: electrical motors, fluorescent lighting, light dimmers, and other communications equipment.

The disparity between the transition regions for inputs and outputs also works as a general safety margin by compensating for some voltage loss in the cable. As much as two volts may be consumed in transit through the cable without the voltage "drooping" into the input's undefined transition zone.

Direct current voltage drops in the cable are usually negligible, however, even for long runs of wire. Since the control and handshaking signals are direct current, they are—in comparison to data signals—relatively unaffected by cable length. For this reason, the RS-232-C standard imposes less rigorous requirements on control signals than on data signals.

Order of Bit Transmission

The data is transmitted "backwards": the *least* significant bit is transmitted first, followed by the others in the reverse order of their significance. Since logic charts (truth tables, bit maps, etc) are customarily drawn with the *most* significant bit on the left, and since western eyes are accustomed to reading from left to right, we naturally tend to visualize bit transmission the same way. That they are transmitted backward has absolutely no significance. It's interesting only as another example of the minor intellectual barriers that must be stepped over in order to visualize what is occurring at the physical level.

Mark and Space

Many people find RS-232-C logical definitions to be perplexing, attributing them, perhaps, to downright orneriness on the part of the

TECHNICAL NOTE:

People are frequently puzzled by the relationships between the speed of data transfer and cable length. Although a full understanding of this topic requires a knowledge of electronics, here is a brief—if slightly technical— explanation.

As the rate of transmission increases, data signals become susceptible to voltage losses caused by capacitance and inductance in the cable. These losses, known as high frequency effects, increase with cable length. By cushioning signal attenuation due to these losses, the width of the transition zone directly limits the maximum rate at which data can be transmitted without degradation.

Since the noise margin is dictated by the RS-232-C standard, the maximum rate of transmission is effectively governed by cable length. And since the amount of voltage loss is related to the length of the cable, the width of the transition region directly determines the maximum distance across which data may be safely transmitted. Exactly how far can you run an RS-232-C cable? The EIA limits the total cable capacitance to 2500 picofarads. Since an average value for cable is 40– 50 picofarads per foot, about 50 feet is the longest distance a cable can possibly run.

The following experiment was performed under less than scientific conditions, but cannot be far off: eleven 250-foot rolls of 3-conductor, unshielded 22 AWG wire were gradually daisy chained during testing into a single cable. A computer's RS-232-C port was connected to each end. A short program was written to the transmit the ASCII "U" at one end of the cable and to receive it from the other end. (The letter "U" was chosen because of its alternating bit pattern: 01010101). The program kept count of errors by tallying any discrepancy between the outgoing and incoming character. The character was transmitted continuously while additional 250-foot lengths were spliced into the line. The length reported is the longest wire length at which the system could transmit about 65,000 characters without error.

BAUD RATE	WIRE LENGTH IN FEET
110	2750
300	2500
600	2500
1200	1750
2400	750
4800	500
9600	250
19200	<250

designers. But, like many aspects of serial communications, conventions such as these can best be understood by looking back at the telegraph and teleprinter technology from which modern practices evolved. Early designers of electromechanical devices (such as the teleprinter) discovered that reliability could be greatly improved by maintaining a fixed current in the transmission line during idle (i.e., when no data is being transmitted). Data transmission was accomplished by interrupting this quiescent current. This idle state (current flowing) was arbitrarily assigned the value 1. In serial communications, this state is also called the MARK condition. Conversely, the absence of current flow (i.e., the actual transmission of data) is defined as 0, or SPACE condition.

The first page of the CCITT document "Data Transmission Over Telephone Networks" makes this historically illuminating point:

> Data transmission on a circuit is often controlled by perforated tape. On perforated tapes used for telegraphy, . . [the MARK] condition is represented by a perforation. When binary numbers are represented by means of perforations, it is customary to represent the symbol 1 with a perforation. It is therefore logical to make this symbol correspond to the . . . [MARK] condition.

If we were to design a general-purpose interface based upon today's logic conventions, we would almost certainly choose the other way. To us, it seems more "logical" that the absence of data (an idling state) should be assigned the logical status of 0 instead of 1. But while tradition ties us inextricably to these inverted definitions, forcing upon us another step in understanding, it also breathes charm and variety into an otherwise deadly, cut-and-dried subject. Thus merely to speak of such things as MARKs and SPACEs is an invitation to recall a refreshing, slightly romantic past.

In addition to the minor mental adjustment required to translate these logic definitions to their conventional equivalents, these inversions are important because of the trouble they cause when people try to explain, write about, or just discuss the RS-232-C interface.

You were earlier cautioned against assigning logic levels to the RS-232-C interface inputs and outputs. This caveat still applies. Because of the confusion engendered by the standard's use of inverted logic, the literature on the subject has become hopelessly inconsistent and confusing. The table in Figure 5.4 summarizes some of the terms in use.

CONTROL AND HANDSHAKING LOGIC LEVELS

As long as we are talking about the logic levels of the actual data, most of the terms in this table make sense. But when control or handshaking signals are discussed, the imprecise language can lead to confusion. For example, the terms "HI" and "LO" are really technical slang derived from modern computer designs where a positive voltage (HI) represents a 1 and near-zero volts (LO) stands for 0. But these distinctions aren't relevant to the RS-232-C interface where a positive voltage represents logic 0, and a negative voltage represents a 1. A similar semantical problem arises because *an output is positive—logic 0— when asserted.* This means, for example, that when **DATA TERMINAL READY** is at logic 0—FALSE—the data terminal *is* ready.

To eliminate these annoying incongruities, it is probably easier to analyze the data lines (**TRANSMITTED DATA** and **RECEIVED DATA**) in terms of inverted logic, but apply conventional logic to the control and handshaking signals. This bit of mental gymnastics is by no means mandatory, but if you have difficulty dealing with the notion that an activated (*enabled*) input is FALSE, it may help.

As a practical matter, though, you can probably forget about the logic inversion altogether. Why? Because virtually all day-to-day interfacing consists of manipulating and tricking control and handshaking lines. Practical interfacing problems will seldom require you to deal

LOGIC 0	LOGIC 1
SPACE	MARK
OFF	ON
START	STOP
FALSE	TRUE
POSITIVE	NEGATIVE
LO	HI
PERFORATION	NO PERFORATION
RESET	SET

—*Figure 5.4: Inverter RS-232-C logic makes use of jargon confusing.*—

with the polarity of the data signals. Since the control and handshaking inputs and outputs obey conventional positive logic (1 = asserted, true, on, and hi), most interfacing problems can be solved using conventional logic.

For our part, we will safely skirt the problem by eschewing TRUE/FALSE, 1/0 altogether in favor of the unambiguous terminology mentioned earlier:

> INPUTS are *enabled* when positive, *disabled* when negative.
>
> OUTPUTS ARE *asserted* when positive, *inhibited* when negative.

Be aware that the manufacturers' documentation can't get these terms straight either. As an illustration, one printer manufacturer imprecisely states "the buffer full signal occurs when pin 20 is false." Experimentation determined that pin 20 became about − 10 volts when the print buffer became full. In the terms set out in the RS-232-C interface standard, the manufacturer's description was not correct: FALSE is a positive voltage! Therefore, the manual could have stated unambiguously that "the buffer full signal occurs when pin 20 becomes *negative*." This sort of linguistic confusion permeates the whole field of RS-232-C documentation, so make certain that you straighten it out in your own mind before trying to figure out how others have misconstrued it.

6

THE INTERFACER'S TOOLKIT

So far we have talked rather academically about the "data flow across the interface," and the fine distinctions between device control logic and handshaking. The stimulating intellectual endeavor of understanding how the interface works is over. We need a few "how to do it" chapters. We're going to be interfacing real equipment with real names, brands, and model numbers. All that remains is work: jumpering pins, tricking inputs, flipping cables. When it gets down to the chore of making two RS-232-C devices function together, the glamourous-sounding "interfacing" suddenly sounds like "cablemaking."

The first step in interfacing is setting the baud rate on both pieces of equipment. Since the baud rate is not a part of the RS-232-C interface *per se*, and the procedure for setting it will differ from device to device, the operator's manuals will have to be consulted for instructions. But after the baud rate is set, we're going to interface our RS-232-C test cases *without* the assistance of manuals. Using simple tools, we will ascertain the logic levels on each piece of equipment, chart them, then make working assumptions based upon what we know about the RS-232-C standard. The initial assumptions will be deductive; that is, by applying tests, we will verify how closely the DTE/DCE, input/output, and electrical specifications contained in the RS-232-C interface standard have been observed. When the devices under test deviate from our expectations, we must then proceed inductively— assembling the pieces of information and looking at the clues to form a new hypothesis about the interface. The results of this analysis will be tested and refined until we have a working interface and, finally, specifications for cabling.

NO DOCUMENTATION

There is nothing more frustrating or futile than working from inadequate or inaccurate documentation. The decision to work without documentation was therefore reached not entirely as a show of bravado, but because manufacturers' manuals are often incorrect, frequently misleading, and always confusing. In some cases, a successful interface can't be achieved relying entirely upon the manuals. Frequently, this is due to the hasty, slap-dash prose that is proffered as documentation, but in a substantial number of the devices tested, the errors revealed a lack of understanding of fundamental RS-232-C interface concepts. Alas, if its equipment were judged solely upon the clarity and precision of its RS-232-C interfacing instructions, the microcomputer industry would be in deep trouble.

SAYS WHO?
DEPARTMENT
The success of a handshake mechanism in an RS-232-C interface cannot be predicted without studying the manuals for both devices involved.
—BYTE, *May 1982*

RS-232-C GROUND RULES

Two RS-232-C electrical specifications permit us to use primitive and unsophisticated techniques for interfacing.

The most important specification for interfacers is almost too good to be true. The EIA standard states:

> The driver on an interchange circuit shall be designed to withstand an open circuit, a short circuit between the conductor carrying that interchange circuit in the interconnecting cable and any other conductor in that cable . . . including Signal Ground, without sustaining damage to itself or its associated equipment.

Any pin may be connected to any other pin at any time without damage. As long as you are interfacing true RS-232-C devices, you can't blow anything up! None of the tests described in this book can harm a genuine RS-232-C interface. Indeed, any interface that cannot withstand our tests is not truly "RS-232-C compatible" (a meager consolation).

Why is this specification such a boon to interfacers? It means that we can indiscriminately jumper pins, share voltages, or short out unwanted voltages—all without hesitation or worry. This safety factor also allows us to make brute-force voltage measurements by connecting *light-emitting diodes* anywhere we like. Thus we can measure logic levels without using voltmeters or other expensive equipment.

A word of caution here: this specification does not mean that the RS-232-C interface is invulnerable to damage. It may, for example, be damaged by connection to any circuit that impresses voltages outside the range of +25 and −25 volts. Be especially wary of home-brew circuitry that appears in hobbyist magazines. Moreover, never assume that the presence of a DB-25 connector guarantees an RS-232-C interface, or even a *serial* interface. Some devices—the IBM PC, for example—use DB-25s for both serial and parallel interface connectors.

The second key specification requires that the transmitter always be at a negative voltage (logic 1, or MARK) when data is not actually being transmitted. We already know that data must be transmitted either upon pins 2 or 3, depending upon the sex of the equipment. Therefore, just by testing these two pins (using an LED) we can ascertain whether the device-under-test is a DTE or a DCE.

Before we assemble our toolkit, you should understand that the procedure described here is intended to interface *healthy* devices that meet RS-232-C electrical and logic level specifications. Although diagnostic information can certainly be deduced from the results of our tests, they were not designed for troubleshooting defective or modified equipment. The procedure may not work where more than one device is daisy-chained to other interfaces (this is known as *multi-drop*). For example, it *may* not be possible to run five printers from the single RS-232-C port on your computer.

TOOLING UP

The Grabber

In the Introduction, we promised that no soldering would be required in order to use the methods in this book. The promise stands. Still, knowing how to solder is of immeasurable help when actually working through the interfacing procedure. The use of spring-loaded wire hooks—clever little devices known as "grabbers"—are recommended as an excellent substitute for soldering. These tools, which are operated much like hypodermic syringes, are pictured in Figure 6.1.

Grabbers are easily found at electronics supply stores. There are two sizes. The hooks on the larger size may be too large to permit attaching two grabbers simultaneously to adjacent pins on a DB-25.

On the other hand, the circumference of the smaller "micrograbber's" hook is too small to grab the pins securely. The hooks on the micrograbber can, however, easily be reformed with a small pair of pliers. If you prefer not to solder wires, six or seven grabbers in various sizes and colors will be necessary. Grabbers can be purchased with wires already installed, or you can buy them in bulk and solder on any length of wires you choose.

Cables And Connectors

No matter whether you decide to solder your connections or to use grabbers, you will soon grow disenchanted with the process of serial interfacing if you try to work on the connectors that are mounted directly upon the equipment. The back panel of computer equipment is not a hospitable working environment because of the snarl of cables and connectors; your inability to see the terminal screen while you work, the lack of lighting, and the physical discomfort of scrunching into a

Soldering seems to be a real bugaboo among nontechnical types. On a scale of sophistication and talent required, soldering is about like hammering nails or perhaps banging out horseshoes on an anvil. What could be easier than heating two strands of wire until they cause solder to melt and flow over them?

While solderless cable connectors do exist, they are frequently difficult

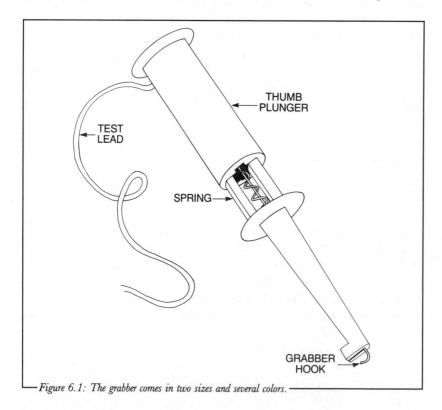

THUMB
PLUNGER

TEST
LEAD

SPRING

GRABBER
HOOK

Figure 6.1: The grabber comes in two sizes and several colors.

to find, inevitably more expensive, and often do not perform reliably. Custom cables cost a fortune. It is safe to say that your soldering iron will more than pay for itself with the money saved by making only one cable.

In an increasingly electronic world, soldering is rapidly becoming a survival skill. The skills can be mastered in about five minutes. Why not learn now?

cramped space. So begin work by connecting a *25 conductor, straight-through cable* (i.e., one without tricks or flips) to each device. Route the cables to a convenient and comfortable work surface where your terminal screen is visible and your keyboard is within easy reach.

Do *not* work directly on the ends of the cable! Instead, with the cables located comfortably on your work surface, install a bare *dummy* connector on the free end of each cable. This will provide a convenient set of pins for soldering or attaching grabber. All test connections are made on the dummy connectors. After you have figured out the interface, the final working cable can then be constructed using the minimum of wires.

If you solder, you may prefer connectors with ordinary solder lugs. If you are using grabbers, the longer lugs of *wire-wrap* connectors provide convenient tie-points onto which grabbers may be attached. The wire-wrap leads may be trimmed to your taste. Figure 6.2 depicts these two types of connectors.

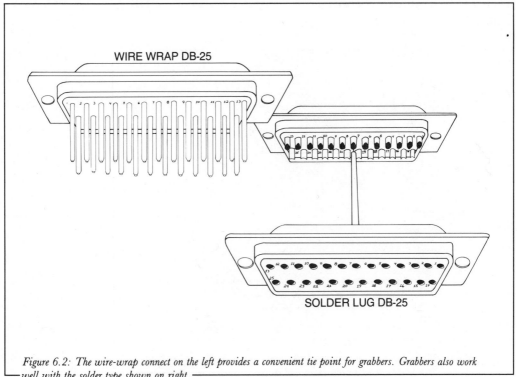

Figure 6.2: The wire-wrap connect on the left provides a convenient tie point for grabbers. Grabbers also work well with the solder type shown on right.

If you begin attaching wires between these dummy DB-25 connectors, the whole apparatus will quickly become floppy and unwieldy. The connectors will be easier to manipulate if they are securely attached to one another to form a *test adaptor*. Threaded spacers about 1 inch long can be used to separate the two connectors, providing a stable platform onto which the grabbers can be connected or wires be soldered. Alternatively, 1½-inch pieces of ordinary 12 gauge house wire can be soldered to the ears of the connectors to hold them in place. Since **CIRCUIT COMMON** pin 7 is *always* required, it is a good idea to solder it *permanently* in place on the test adaptor as shown in Figure 6.3.

If you construct your test adaptor with spacers, be sure to use binder-head or flat-head screws to secure the spacers between the DB-25's; screws with large heads will prevent the connector on the cable from seating securely over the adaptor. For the same reason, when constructing your adaptor from 12 gauge wire, do *not* pass the wire through the holes on the connectors. Using lengths of 12 gauge wire about 1½ inches long, bend over ¼ inch of wire at 90° at each end. Then solder the wires to the metal frame on the *underside* of the DB-25 connectors.

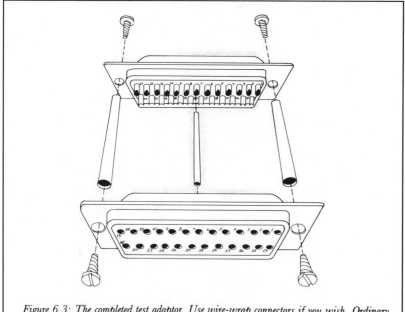

Figure 6.3: The completed test adaptor. Use wire-wrap connectors if you wish. Ordinary 12 gauge wire may be substituted for the screws and spacers.

It is a good idea to mount both connectors on the test adaptor so that their "D" outlines are oriented the same. This assures that the pins on one connector will line up directly across from the pins of the same number on the other connector. Otherwise, it is possible—depending upon the sex of the connectors—that the locations of the pin numbers will be inverted. Since it is dangerously easy to misidentify pins on opposite-facing connectors—a fatal error—it is a good idea to label the connector apron with the numbers of the BIG EIGHT pins (use a fine-tipped indelible marker).

By constructing three adaptors—male/male, male/female, and female/female—only one kind of cable (a male/female) is needed in your test kit, regardless of the sex of the connectors on the equipment being interfaced. The adaptors therefore serve the dual function of providing a stable work platform and reducing the number of cables required.

Alternatively, you may choose to employ a *universal cable,* one with a male and female connector on *both* ends. A universal cable, a single male/female test adaptor, and a single male/female cable will cover all contingencies.

THE QUICK-AND-DIRTY LED VOLTAGE DETECTOR

Because the RS-232-C interface uses binary logic, we are more concerned with the mere presence or absence of a signal than with its magnitude. Previously, we learned that an input's "logical trippoints" were +3 volts and −3 volts. Whether the voltages are greater (more negative or more positive) is unimportant. In fact, in practical applications, most equipment will work fine with logic levels of about

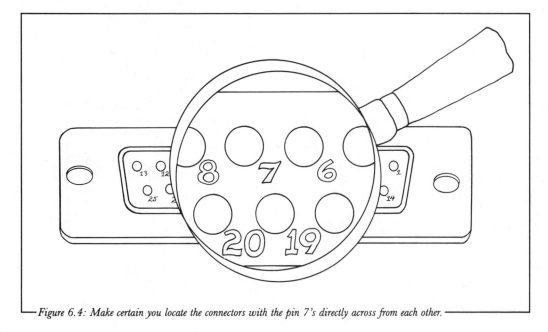

Figure 6.4: Make certain you locate the connectors with the pin 7's directly across from each other.

+1 and −1. (Remember, however, that the interface doesn't *guarantee* logic levels less than ±3 volts will work.)

To aid in our analysis of interfaces, a simple tester must be devised to monitor the presence or absence of the pin voltages. In addition to detecting the minimum 3 volt level, this tester should be able to detect voltage polarity; that is, it must indicate whether a voltage is negative or positive.

The light-emitting diode, or LED, is perfect for the job. Like all diodes, the LED responds only to voltages of one polarity. Figure 6.5 illustrates this unique property.

We will utilize this phenomenon to indicate whether pins on the RS-232-C interface are positive or negative. Notice that one leg on the LED is shorter than the other and that there is a flat spot on the brim of the lens. These features mark the negative terminal of the LED. If this lead is connected to the **CIRCUIT COMMON** pin 7 on the RS-232-C interface and the other lead to any pin with a *positive* voltage

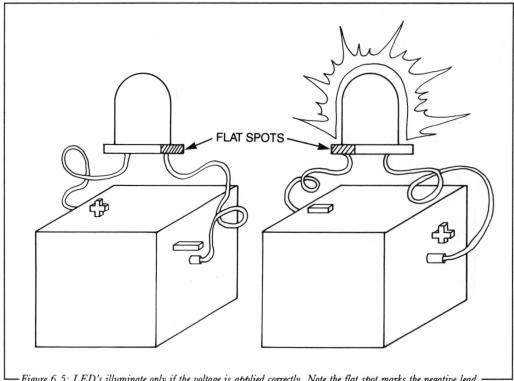

Figure 6.5: LED's illuminate only if the voltage is applied correctly. Note the flat spot marks the negative lead.

(i.e., asserted), the LED will glow. Fortunately, when it is not glowing, the LED has absolutely no effect upon the interface circuitry. Figure 6.6 shows an LED tester complete with grabbers.

An identical tester for negative voltages can be constructed simply by reversing the LED connections so that the *positive* lead is now connected to **CIRCUIT COMMON** pin 7. Now the LED will glow only when the interface pin under test is negative. Since a voltage cannot be simultaneously positive and negative, and since an extinguished LED doesn't affect the voltages on the interface, there is no reason why we can't combine two LEDs of different colors to create a bipolar voltage detector.

If the lead marked COMMON is connected to **CIRCUIT COMMON,** the red LED will glow when a positive voltage is applied to the lead marked TEST. If a negative voltage is applied, the green LED will illuminate.

Figure 6.7 shows the finished voltage tester, complete with a 470 ohm, ½ watt current limiting resistor. Be certain that the green LED's flat spot is opposite the red's. It is strongly recommended that the resistor-diode assembly be soldered; you may also elect to solder the grabber wires to the assembly.

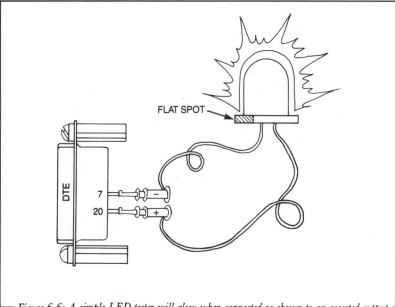

Figure 6.6: A simple LED tester will glow when connected as shown to an asserted output.

A single, two-colored LED may also be used. Since there is no convention to tell you which color will be illuminated with a given hookup, you will have to determine experimentally which of its leads must be connected to **CIRCUIT COMMON.** The 470 ohm resistor will still be required.

The toolkit is now complete: grabbers, test adaptor, and voltage tester. Excluding cables (which you may already own), the cost for a single test adaptor, six grabbers, and the LED tester should be well under $15. It's now time to combine these physical tools with the mental tools acquired in previous chapters.

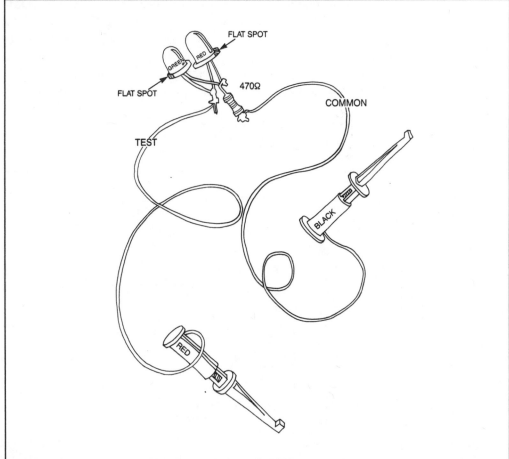

Figure 6.7: The completed LED tester. The value of the 470 Ω may vary ±20%. The TEST lead connects to the non-flat side of the red LED and to the flat side of the green LED.

TEST CONNECTOR PARTS (for 3* units):

3   Male connectors
3   Female connectors
6   #4 × ¼ binder-head screws
6   #4 × 1-¼ threaded spacers or lengths of #12 gauge wire

LED TESTER

1   470 ohm, ½ resistor (value not critical)
1   green light-emitting diode
1   red light-emitting diode or a single two-color light-emitting diode
2   6-12 inch wires with grabbers on one end if soldered, on both sides if not soldered.

MISCELLANEOUS

2   male/female 25-pin, straight-through cables*
6   test wires, grabbers of various colors on each end. If you wire your own grabbers, try to purchase 24 gauge *test lead* wire.

If a universal cable is substituted for one of the male/female cables, only a single male/female test adaptor is required.

Figure 6.8: Parts list for toolkit

STEP-BY-STEP INTERFACING

Good News

We described our printer and our computer as "mythical," in part because—as you may have noticed—it will work fine with a standard, straight-through cable. The printer's (DTE) buffer full signal is asserted on pin 4, **REQUEST TO SEND**. Pin 4 on the interface is connected directly to SPECIAL-PURPOSE INPUT #1, pausing the computer's transmitter. Since the printer is not sending data back to the computer (i.e., is not software handshaking), back to the computer, we have seen how the **REQUEST TO SEND** (**RTS**) and

RECEIVED DATA lines are theoretically superfluous. It is a plausible interface, remaining straightforward while only slightly stretching the RS-232-C interface standard. Even the name of the handshaking line, **REQUEST TO SEND,** is suggestive of what's going on.

Bad News

Before this rosy optimism goes too far, it is time to confess that there is scarce hope that our interface will work on many real printer/computer combinations. Here's why:

1. Few printers signal buffer full on pin 4 (RTS).
2. Half the computers will be configured as DTE devices.
3. Of the computers configured DCE, only a few will connect the **SPECIAL-PURPOSE INPUT #1** of their UARTs to pin 4 (**REQUEST TO SEND**).

While our hypothetical interface will not be of much value in the real-world example of RS-232-C interfacing, it nicely illustrates the processes by which two devices are interfaced. In the next five chapters, we will apply these general ideas to several case studies, applying the principles derived from our hypothetical interface to actual devices, working our way through the problems presented by oddball devices, sex incompatibilities, and manufacturers' "creative" interfacing in general. Here's a succinct outline of how our interfacing will proceed:

1. Set baud rate
2. Ascertain the sex of the equipment
3. Satisfy device control logic
4. Locate the handshaking
5. Specify the cable

GENERAL CONSIDERATIONS

In each study we will begin with general information, presenting important facts, or providing preliminary explanations to new topics.

Before worrying about interfacing two pieces of RS-232-C equipment, don't hesitate to connect them with a straight-through cable and give it a try. You've nothing to lose: even the grossest mismatch imaginable won't harm either piece of equipment.

Remember, not all equipment will need both device control and handshaking. Modems, for example, require device control, but need no handshaking. Terminals frequently require neither. Much of the necessary flipping and tricking can be done with internal switches. Manufacturers have recently begun to install switches intended to defeat device control requirements altogether. Some printers and modems even provide a switch for flipping the **TRANSMITTED DATA** and **RECEIVED DATA** lines.

Set The Baud Rate

When parallel data bits are disassembled, they are transmitted across the interface at a precise speed, or *bit rate*. Under most conditions, bit rate is synonymous with the more familiar term *baud rate*. On the receiving end, the bits must, of course, be reassembled at *very* near this rate. This process may be visualized as an old-fashioned bucket brigade, with the transmitting interface handing bits to the receiving interface. If the baud rate is set at a speed unattainable by either device, or if the two devices are operating at widely different baud rates, the data will probably move across the interface, but will become garbled in some way. Errors in baud rate may cause characters transmitted in variety to be received identically or as a mixture of incorrect characters. In cases of extreme baud rate mismatch, however, the receiving device may appear not to be receiving data at all. For this reason, setting the baud rates must be the first step. Otherwise, a refusal to pass data because of a simple baud rate mismatch might be mistaken for device control or handshaking problems.

Baud rate may be selected in several ways. First, it may be selected by changing the position of one or more switches inside the device. Second, the baud rate on computers may respond only to software commands, in which case it will be necessary to run a *configuration program*. Such programs generally present the user with a menu from which the desired baud rate may be chosen. On some equipment, it may be necessary to set the baud rate switches *and* run a configuration program in order to achieve the desired baud rate. Some "intelligent" equipment automatically figures out the baud rate of an incoming data stream, and adjust its own baud rate to match.

Additional details about this subject will be introduced as they become relevant, so for the present, regard the setting of the baud rate as just one of five checkpoints to successful interfacing.

Ascertain The Sex of The Devices

Another name for this step might be "locate the data signals." This heading was chosen because it emphasizes how locating the transmitter provides a wealth of other, supplementary information. As you become more familiar with the procedure, you will find that the distinctions between steps blur.

The sex of a device may be determined experimentally simply by discovering on which pins it receives or transmits. Any device that transmits on pin 2 or receives on pin 3 is, by definition, a DTE. A DCE will do the opposite. If two devices have the same sex, one must be changed ("flipped") so that its inputs and outputs complement those of the other device. You'll learn exactly how to do this in the case studies.

Satisfy The Control Logic

Our basic approach will always be to trick both sides of the interface, one at a time, in order to determine what is required to stimulate transmission or enable reception of data. Remember, control logic does not regulate the flow of data—it just makes it possible. This step is successfully accomplished when *both* devices are able to transfer data, although the data itself may be garbled, distorted, or otherwise unsatisfactory. For example, when interfacing a printer and a microcomputer, your first task will be to make the printer print *something* upon command. You don't care if it prints all question marks or a's, or if the wrong characters are always printed. Once the printer is *able* to print, the control logic portion of the interface is working correctly.

Don't hesitate to trick *every* control and handshaking input on both ends of the cable. At this stage, you are not interested in establishing controlled data flow, just in getting the data to move at all.

As we have seen, whenever control logic is used, it is usually implemented through the **DATA TERMINAL READY/DATA SET READY** and **REQUEST TO SEND/CLEAR TO SEND** signals.

Locate The Handshaking

While control logic enables the flow of data, handshaking actually regulates and controls it. As we have seen, this occurs when one device signals the other that certain conditions have occurred. The signaled device then changes its behavior based upon a predetermined interpretation of the signal. Our printer, for example, signals that its print buffer is full by inhibiting a pin on the RS-232-C interface. At the computer end, this inhibition eventually causes the UART to interrupt the flow of data through its transmitter. So, after satisfaction of the control logic, our next goal is simply to identify the pin on each device that is dedicated to handshaking.

As we noted earlier, some devices provide handshaking to disable their receivers as well as their transmitters. This handshake *input* is usually connected to pin 8, **DATA CARRIER DETECT**. Receiver interruption is often found on devices that are designed for remote control through modems. Some printers, for example, will require an enabled **dcd** before they will do *anything*. It is important not to mistake this ordinary control logic for a handshaking problem.

Specify The Cable

The entire process of satisfying the handshaking, then, may be simplified to mean locating the pin on the controll*ing* device that generates the handshaking output signal, locating the pin on the controll*ed* device that inputs the handshaking signal, then connecting the two.

After the devices are actively and successfully handshaking, you may remove the tricks installed during the *satisfy the control logic* phase. Sometimes these tricks will only have defeated a trivial function— power-up handshaking, for example. The rule is simple: if the disabled control logic doesn't control anything of value to you, leave the tricks in place. If you do remove the tricks, remove them one at a time, testing the interface after each one is removed.

With each case study, we will proceed according to this outline, adding embellishments and refinements as necessary. The basic goal of these case studies, aside from providing some real information on popular computers, is to build a generalized, works-every-time formula for interfacing any two RS-232-C devices. Since the RS-232-C interface is binary, the entire process can be represented by a *flowchart*. Within the constraints of our 5-step outline, we'll develop such a chart as we work through the various case studies.

"START YOUR ENGINES!"

We have now looked at the RS-232-C interface from the perspective of a conceptual device for passing electrical impulses between digital equipment. We have looked at it from the perspective of the UART, the device that is actually running the show. In between, we've seen another layer of devices used to convert UART voltages into the voltages defined by the RS-232-C standard.

Along the way, we've seen that certain kinds of interfacing—devices of opposite sexes, for example—can cause consternation. To solve these problems, we've developed a trickbag to allow us to interface devices not officially supported by the RS-232-C standard. Voltage/logic levels have been treated and terminology explained.

All that remains is to study some real live examples of interfacing, but before taking the plunge, here's a bit of free philosophy. The process is best undertaken in the spirit of unravelling a good mystery or solving a riddle. A sense of humor helps, too. After only a few tries, you'll almost be able to *sense* how an interface is designed to work. You'll soon find yourself recognizing familiar input/output patterns and their implications. Best of all, the results are always gratifying—you've made things work.

Although the charts in the following chapters were developed from real equipment, don't be surprised if you find that they do not correspond to the information you get from different units, even though they have identical model numbers. Manufacturers frequently alter the design of their serial ports, reflecting price changes in UARTs or other hardware. In addition, the serial interface in your equipment may not be manufactured by the maker of your computer. For example, there are at least 20 manufacturers of serial I/O boards for the IBM PC. The logic charts and cable diagrams that you derive may therefore be totally different from the ones shown here.

Part II

SB80/ADDS
CASE STUDY 1:

COLONIAL DATA SB80 Computer (s/n 305-1):CP/M
Single-board computer
ADVANCED DIGITAL DATA SYSTEMS VIEW-
POINT Terminal (s/n 698901)

GENERAL INFORMATION

This terminal is intended for use as the CP/M logical console device (**CON:**). A console terminal has dual functions: it translates keystrokes into parallel characters, converts them to a stream of serial bits, then dispatches them from the RS-232-C port. In this role, the UART transmitter section is employed. When it is not transmitting characters, the terminal must also monitor the receiver section of the UART to catch any character sent its way by the computer. The computer, of course, performs complementary functions: receiving the characters sent from the terminal, and outputting characters bound for the terminal's screen.

Though the subjects of our first case study are hardly household brand names, this pair have earned their place in this book—they were used to write it.

Step 1: Set The Baud Rate

The SB-80's console serial port is set to 9600 baud by the CP/M operating system. 9600 baud is a de facto standard for terminals, although most terminals and computers will work fine at 19,200 baud (the maximum speed allowed by the RS-232-C interface standard). The terminal's baud rate is set to 9600 baud by a bank of micro-switches on the back panel.

Step 2: Ascertain The Sex of the Equipment

Our first task will be to determine the sex of the computer's serial port. The fact that it's designed by the computer manufacturer to interface with a terminal device is by no means any guarantee that it will be a DCE.

The computer and terminal are both connected via 25-pin male/male cables to a female/female test adaptor. Pin 7 is already connected on the adaptor. We will ascertain the sex of the computer first. How? Connect the bipolar LED tester's TEST lead to either pin 7 on the test adaptor, then connect the TEST lead to the computer side's pin 2. If this is a DTE device, pin 2 should be the transmitter, and its negative voltage will illuminate the green LED. As noted above, under the RS-232-C interface standard, an idling transmitter must show a negative voltage (MARKing). The receiver's input voltage is not specified.

When the tester was applied to the computer's **TxD (TRANSMITTED DATA)** pin 2, however, the green LED did not glow.

Do not assume that since the device is not a DTE, it must automatically be a DCE. On the contrary, it could be a non-RS-232-C interface that just happens to use a DB-25 connector. Pin 3 must be tested for a negative voltage, just to be sure. Pin 3 illuminated the green LED.

We have now determined that the computer uses pin 3 as a transmitter and therefore must be a DCE device. This part of the testing procedure is summarized by the flowchart in Figure 7.1.

The flowchart represents tests with rectangles, while questions are shown in diamonds. A *branch* is made to the next test depending on the answer to the YES/NO question. The branching process is repeated until some logical conclusion is reached. In our case, one of four conclusions is possible: our device under test may be a DTE, a DCE, or neither. Or it may be an RS-232-C device without a transmitter. Recall, for example, that many printers have no need to transmit data. When no transmitter is present, then, this test is inconclusive, but most of the time, the remainder of the interface chart will clearly announce the sex of the device. Peruse the flowchart until you understand the logical processes it schematically represents.

In an identical fashion, the terminal was tested. Here, however, the green LED illuminated on pin 2—the terminal is a DTE.

Since the two devices are complementary, flipping—or at least *large-scale* flipping—should not be required.

Step 3: Satisfy the Control Logic

As before, we'll test the computer side first. Before we can satisfy the control logic, we must first chart it. This, too, is done with the LED tester. As always, its COMMON lead is connected to pin 7. One by one, every pin on the connector is logged on the following chart. There are three possibilities:

1. Negative—green LED illuminates
2. Positive—red LED illuminates
3. Transition—neither LED illuminates

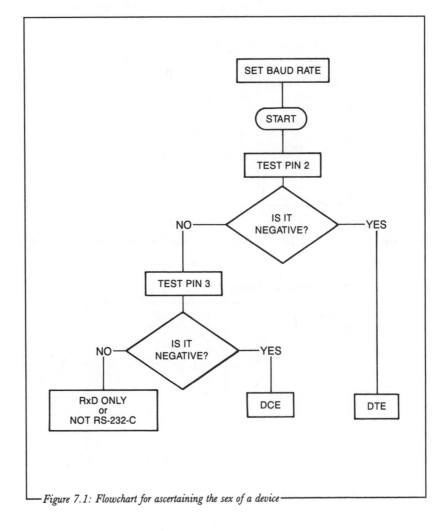

Figure 7.1: Flowchart for ascertaining the sex of a device

We will use NEG to stand for negative, POS for positive. Inactive pins that illuminate neither LED should *not* be left blank—otherwise, you may not know whether you've measured zero volts or simply neglected to test the pin. Instead, use an X to represent any undefined logic state. Beside each pin number is the abbreviation of its name as well as the familiar ! for an output and ? for an input. When the connector is charted, you'll have a good idea of what control logic is being used. In Figure 7.2 you'll see the chart for the computer.

To avoid confusion, our charts will always show the status of the seven pins shown above. In the interest of tidiness, other *inactive* pins will not be shown. Figure 7.3 shows the chart for the terminal.

DCE :   SB-80 COMPUTER, Console port

PIN	I/O	VOLTS TEST
2 TxD	?	X
3 RxD	!	NEG
4 RTS	?	X
5 CTS	!	POS
6 DSR	!	X
8 DCD	!	X
20 DTR	?	X

——*Figure 7.2: Logic chart for SB-80 computer, console port*———————————————————

DTE: ADDS A2 Terminal

PIN	I/O	VOLTS TEST
2 TxD	!	NEG
3 RxD	?	X
4 RTS	!	POS
5 CTS	?	X
6 DSR	?	X
8 DCD	?	X
11 —		POS
20 DTR	!	POS

——*Figure 7.3: Logic chart for ADDS terminal*———————————————————

In order to determine if the terminal's control logic is satisfied, we must now attempt to make it perform its transmit and receive functions. What kind of test is available for a terminal? Since the terminal contains both a transmitter and a receiver, there's no reason why pins 2 and 3 cannot be connected to each other. This is known as a *loop-back* test. If the control logic is satisfactory, any characters you type on the keyboard should appear directly on the screen.

This RxD/TxD jumpering is pictured in Figure 7.4.

When jumpered as described above, the ADDS terminal's keyboard characters are correctly *echoed* back to the screen.

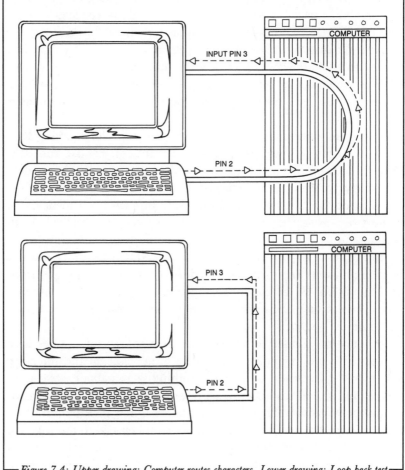

Figure 7.4: Upper drawing: Computer routes characters. Lower drawing: Loop back test

This result tempts us to declare the analysis complete. After all, if the device works, who cares about the input and output voltage? Before we jump to such a presumptive conclusion, we must first ascertain if any of the control inputs is *active*—that is, whether it will affect data flow when it's disabled. Unfortunately, when the LED tester fails to indicate the presence of a voltage (of either polarity) on an unconnected active input, we cannot be certain whether the input is enabled or disabled.

This problem of input ambiguity appears to be an oversight in the RS-232-C interface standard: the logic state of an unconnected, active input is *not* specified. To illustrate this shortcoming, recall that if we test one of the outputs—DTR on the terminal, for example—it will be *either* positive *or* negative. If it is nonexistent, we can consider it to be irrelevant. There is no such specification for input voltages. As discussed in Chapter 5, unless an input voltage is in the ± 3 volt range, there is no absolute way to predict if the input is enabled or disabled. When active inputs are left unconnected, they are known as *open inputs* or *floating inputs*. We'll adopt the term "open input" for the remainder of this book.

Look again at the chart for the ADDS terminal. Not counting **RxD** pin 3, there are *at least* three open DTE inputs: **cts,dsr**,and **dcd**. Because the DTE side of the interface both transmits and receives data successfully, we may conclude that, despite their absence of voltage, all active inputs are interpreted as enabled. But we need to devise a method to *guarantee* that an input is either enabled or disabled. With each input thus disabled, we can judge if it affects the data transfer.

Pretend, as a hypothetical case, that the ADDS terminal will not function unless its **dsr** input is enabled. Still with the test jumper from pin 2 to pin 3, if we disable **dsr** by applying a negative voltage of more than -3 volts, then characters typed at the keyboard should no longer appear on the screen.

You may be wondering what to use as a source for the negative voltage. The only negative voltage on either side of the interface belongs to the transmitters. There is nothing sacred about a transmitter's output . . . we can borrow its negative voltage just as we might borrow the negative voltage from, say, an inhibited **DTR** output. This is accomplished by attaching one end of a grabber lead to the negative transmitter lead while applying the other end of the grabber to an ambiguous input pin. As each pin is jumpered, a few characters are typed on the keyboard to see if they arrive at the screen. Remember, an RS-232-C interface cannot be damaged by shorting its pins, so don't worry if you accidentally touch the transmitter lead to one of the asserted output pins. (Keep in mind, however, that if the transmitter is connected to another *output*, it probably will not transmit.)

Every ambiguous pin on the connector must be tested in this way: apply a negative voltage to the pins one by one; if the data flow stops, the input is, by definition, active. On the other hand, if the negative voltage has no effect, the pin is simply an unused pin and may thereafter be ignored.

Make your own chart, and under TEST RESULTS, note the effect of this process of applying the disabling negative voltage. Make this test on *all ambiguous pins*. Of course, if an interface supplies a negative voltage besides the transmitter pin, feel free to use it instead.

Back to the ADDS terminal. When its **cts** pin 5 is made negative, it will not operate. Neither **dsr** pin 6 nor any of the other twenty-two pins affects its operation. We know that this side of the interface "expects" to receive a control signal on pin 5 **cts**. This requirement must be addressed when specifying the cable.

To test the Colonial Data SB-80 computer's side of the interface, we begin by removing the test jumper from the terminal and, using grabbers, connect pins 2 and 3 on the terminal to pin 2 and pin 3 on the computer. With just the TxD and RxD pins connected, the computer and terminal work fine together.

Applying the identical procedure used on the terminal, the negative voltage from one of the pins is applied by grabber to each ambiguous pin on the computer's interface. When this negative voltage is applied to an active input, the flow of data from the computer will be interrupted and the typed characters will not be displayed on the screen.

When this test was performed on the SB-80, no active pins were found.

We now have all the information necessary to interface the computer to the terminal. For a complete perspective, Figure 7.5 shows a combination of the two charts side by side.

What about pin 11? Since it's not defined in the RS-232-C interface standard, who knows what its purpose is here? We can regard it as a general-purpose output, and otherwise ignore it.

In Figure 7.6, the process of satisfying control logic is translated into a simple flowchart.

Step 4: Locate The Handshaking

There is generally no handshaking between a terminal and a computer. Since each device is capable of handling characters at the maximum allowable speed (19,200 baud), handshaking is unnecessary.

Step 5: Specify The Cable

Figure 7.5 shows the pins necessary to interface the terminal and computer. **CIRCUIT COMMON** pin 7 must be included in the cable. Pin 2 **TRANSMITTED DATA** and pin 3 **RECEIVED DATA** are also required.

But what to do with the terminal's **CLEAR TO SEND** pin 5 input? It obviously works just fine when left open. Should we bother with something that already works? *Yes,* repeat, *yes.* According to the definition contained within the RS-232-C interface standard, an open input is an ambiguous input. With current design practices using current integrated circuits, you can probably expect an open input to behave as an enabled input *most* of the time. But this is entirely too iffy. Neglecting to disable unused active inputs on peripheral equipment is the chief cause of "phantom" failure—a printer that mysteriously stops, then starts again, or a modem that momentarily won't transmit.

The first axiom of interfacing is "assume nothing unnecessarily," and its first corollary is "leave nothing to chance." This reasoning must apply to our open **cts** input pin 5. While it is true that most interfaces will function perfectly with open active inputs, nothing in the interfacing standard requires them to do so. Besides, since the remedy

DTE: ADDS A2 Terminal   DCE: SB-80 Computer

TEST RESULTS		I/O	PIN #	I/O	TEST RESULTS
	NEG	!	2 TxD	?	X
	X	?	3 RxD	!	NEG
	POS	!	4 RTS	?	X
ACTIVE	X	?	5 CTS	!	POS
	X	?	6 DSR	!	X
	X	?	8 DCD	!	X
	POS	–	11 ----	–	X
	POS	!	20 DTR	?	X

Figure 7.5: Combined logic chart for SB-80 and ADDS terminal

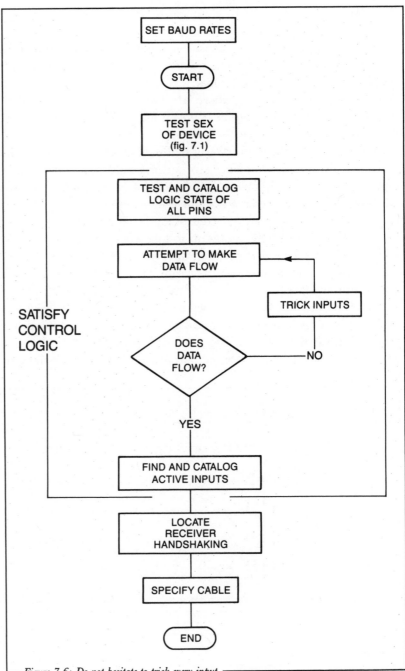

Figure 7.6: Do not hesitate to trick every input.

is so simple, why leave it to chance? *All unused active inputs must be disabled.*

Although it would be an expensive solution, a straight-through 25-pin cable will work just fine. The positive voltage on DCE's pin 5 will enable the **cts** input on the terminal.

With homemade cables, there are two ways to deal with the requirement that the **cts** input be enabled. Figure 7.7 shows the pin 5's connected through the cable.

With this cable, the terminal will be disabled when its pin 5 is disabled. Using this mechanism, a program could suspend terminal input for some special application. At any rate, the control logic on **CLEAR TO SEND** is preserved with a 4-wire cable.

Much of the time, however, control logic will not be important to the application. It's rarely important to take your terminal off-line by control logic. Realistically speaking, any software that would turn off the terminal via **CTS** could just as easily ignore the terminal's serial port altogether. In cases like this one, then, the control logic is of trivial value and the problem of an open active **cts** input can be solved by constructing a 3-wire cable with a *pull-up* jumper on the terminal's pin 5. A pull-up is merely a trick to guarantee (as opposed to defeat) a logic state. Any one of the asserted outputs can be used for pulling up

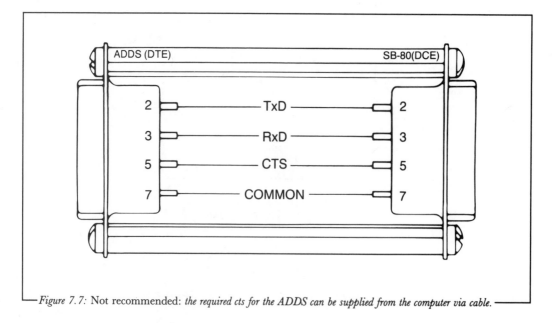

Figure 7.7: Not recommended: *the required cts for the ADDS can be supplied from the computer via cable.*

the **cts** input, but since **RTS** pin 4 is closest, it's the usual choice. Figure 7.8 illustrates the 3-wire cable with pull-up.

Luckily, 25 pin cables are hardly ever required with microcomputers. Made-to-order cables—even those with just a few wires—can be exorbitantly expensive. Generally speaking, cables can be hand-made for about ten percent of their purchase price. This disparity grows even larger when comparing a store-bought 25-pin cable with a homemade one that uses only a few lines.

As you work through the remaining case studies, note that, in addition to the financial penalty, the use of all 25 wires can actually *prevent* proper operation of an interface.

COMMENTS

After successfully interfacing equipment without the assistance of operator's manuals, it is always interesting to look back at them.

The Colonial Data SB80's manual, for example, contains this garden of misinformation for interfacing a serial printer:

> In the *standard* DCE arrangement . . . RTS is output
> to pin 5 and CTS is input from pin 4. DTR is output to

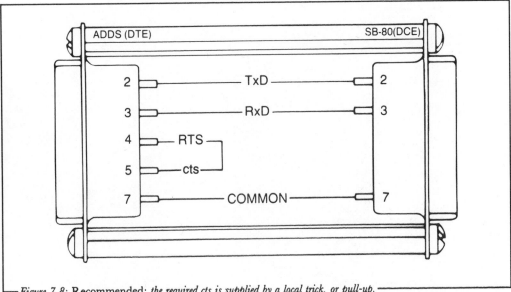

Figure 7.8: Recommended: *the required cts is supplied by a local trick, or pull-up.*

pin 8 and DCD is input from pin 20. These may be changed to the *standard* DTE arrangement by simply interchanging the respective pairs.

This statement is wrong in just about every possible area. First, what does the word *standard* refer to here? Second, the names of the pins do not change with the sex of a device—only their functions. Third, DCD and DTR are not an input/output pair.

8

N*/OKI CASE STUDY 2:

NORTHSTAR ADVANTAGE COMPUTER: integrated computer running CP/M (SN 026873)
OKIDATA PRINTER MICROLINE 83A: serial/parallel dot matrix printer (SN 143161)

GENERAL INFORMATION

The study of printers thrusts us into the subject of "buffer full" handshaking as described in Chapter 3. This interfacing experience has been traditionally so unpleasant that users frequently abandon hardware handshaking and resort to the use of software handshaking. This is a mistake. Not all operating systems support software handshaking. This means that it will not be possible to operate the printer as a peripheral device under the control of the operating system. (Under CP/M, you would lose the ability to send screen output to your printer.) True, various application programs—such as word processors—will drive your printer with their internal software handshaking routines. Most CP/M programs, however, expect your printer to be interfaced through hardware handshaking. Put another way, you can run *any* printer application from CP/M if your printer uses hardware handshaking. Software handshaking should be considered only when the equipment cannot be directly connected by a cable (such as when operating a printer via a modem), or in the rare instance when a printer can't hardware handshake.

The Northstar Advantage supports a variety of serial or parallel ports by plug-in cards. Although the CP/M operating system is not supplied with the Advantage, it is available as an option. The CP/M LST: device defaults to the card in slot #1.

Step 1: Set The Baud Rate

A printer should never have to wait for data to be sent from a computer. Since the Okidata printer will print 120 characters per second, it should be fed data *at least* this fast. 120 cps works out to about 1200 baud. Since 1200 baud is the highest rate available on the 83A (a high-speed serial interface is optional), it was chosen.

The Okidata printer contains both a parallel and a serial interface. The serial interface and its baud rate are selected by internal micro-switches.

In order to match the printer, the Advantage's baud rate was set at 1200 by means of the program CPMGEN.COM supplied with Northstar's CP/M.

Step 2: Ascertain the Sex of the Equipment

Step 3: Satisfy the Control Logic

Two steps have been consolidated. Charting the logic levels and determining the sex of the devices, though intellectually distinct, can actually be accomplished in one step. For the sake of consistency, we will continue to list all steps.

Using the LED tester and the procedure developed in the Case Study 1, the chart in Figure 8.1 was compiled.

This pair presents a more interesting interfacing picture than the computer and terminal from Case Study 1. Let's examine the printer first to see what can be inferred from its logic chart. First, we can see that the printer has no transmitter—neither pin 2 nor pin 3 is negative.

DTE: OKIDATA 83A   DCE: NORTHSTAR ADVANTAGE

TEST RESULTS	I/O	PIN #	I/O	TEST RESULTS
X	!	2 TxD	?	X
X	?	3 RxD	!	NEG
NEG	!	4 RTS	?	X
X	?	5 CTS	!	POS
X	?	6 DSR	!	POS
X	?	8 DCD	!	POS
POS	–	11 —	–	
POS	!	20 DTR	?	POS

Figure 8.1: The Okidata/Northstar logic Chart

(This means that this printer would not software handshake because it can't send data.) But without the negative voltage to mark the transmitter pin, how can we be sure that the printer is a DTE? Well, thankfully, printers are almost always DTEs. Aside from that rule, there is scant evidence. The positive voltage on pin 20 and the negative voltage on pin 4 usually indicate outputs. We'll be able to test this hypothesis easily by finding out if the printer accepts data on pin 3.

The negative **RTS** pin 4 is bit perplexing: is it an inhibited output? We'll find out during the **FIND AND CATALOG ACTIVE INPUTS** phase of interfacing. If we can find no circumstance under which this pin becomes asserted (perhaps it is used to signal "out of paper"), or if making it negative doesn't affect the flow of data in any way, we can safely ignore it when we specify the cable.

There's also that asserted pin 11 again. Pins 11, 18, and 25 are left unassigned in the RS-232-C interface standard. Pins 9 and 10 are, as the standard states, "reserved for Data Set Testing." (Data Set is the telephone company's jargon for "modem," hence the term "data set ready.") Unassigned pins are good candidates for handshaking leads. This will be one of the first places we'll look to find the pin the Okidata uses to signal a full buffer.

Now let's discuss the Advantage's side of the chart. Notice that the negative voltage on **TxD** pin 3 makes the Advantage an unambiguous DCE. The **rts** input is open. We'll need to find out if it is active. The DCE outputs **CTS**, **DSR**, and **DCD** are all asserted. The only slightly suspicious thing here is that **dtr**, a DCE input, is positive. Perhaps it is pulled up internally. That's a big clue: when a designer goes to the trouble to pull up an input, it's almost certain to be active. **DTR**, then, is a good candidate to be the pin that interrupts the Advantage's transmitter—its handshaking pin.

Sending Data to the Printer with CP/M's LST: DEVICE

According to our plan, we need to get each individual piece of equipment to pass data. Since the printer's data must come from the computer, we'll concentrate on tricking the Advantage into transmission. But how do we make the Advantage output characters to the serial printer port? In CP/M, all characters bound for the screen can also be sent to the printer (more precisely, the **LST:** device). Data flow to the printer is *toggled*—turned on and off—by alternately pressing control-P. Inside CP/M, as each character is sent to the screen, it is immediately sent to the printer. Transmitting data to the printer, in effect, limits the speed of the screen display to the printer port's baud rate: characters can be sent to the screen no faster than they can be dispatched to the printer! This feature is implemented on virtually every CP/M computer and, in some form, on most others as well.

But pretend that the Advantage UART's transmitter is interrupted by a disabled (or even ambiguous) handshaking line. Unless this handshaking pin is enabled, the screen output will not occur—CP/M just patiently waits for the UART's OK to transmit the next character, and, as long as the handshaking line is inhibited, the OK is never given. The screen, then, is a built-in data flow tester. We can tell if CP/M is transmitting characters by "control-P-ing" the printer on, then typing a command that sends data to the screen. If the handshaking input is enabled, all screen activity will print on the screen *at the printer's baud rate*. But when the handshaking line is disabled, the screen display will cease altogether! We'll use this powerful feature as an important interfacing tool.

When the Advantage's printer is turned on with a control-P and **DIR** is typed, the display prints out the **A:** drive's directory at 1200 baud, the printer's baud rate.

This tells us that wherever the Advantage's handshaking input pin may be, it is *enabled* (or ambiguous). But before we go in search of the handshaking line, let's apply the test for active inputs by jumpering them one by one to a negative voltage. Here's a good use for that negative voltage on the Okidata **RTS** pin 4. (Any time you use a single pin from the other device, make certain that their commons are connected. This is why we recommended that the pin 7's be permanently soldered on the test adaptor.) To perform this test, the printer is engaged with a control-P and a long text file is listed to the screen with the command **TYPE FILENAME.EXT**. While keeping one eye on the screen, a grabber jumper is attached between the negative **RTS** pin 4 on the Okidata and each pin on the Advantage's interface.

Applying a negative voltage to the **rts** pin 4 input has no effect on the data going to the screen. However, when **dtr** pin 20 is made negative, the screen freezes. Remove the negative voltage and the output resumes. **dtr** pin 20, then, is the only active input on the Advantage side of the interface. It is, by default, the handshaking input we are looking for.

Step 4: Locate the Handshaking

The next task is to force the Okidata to print characters on paper. As a first attempt, the Advantage's transmitter is connected to the Okidata's receiver by jumpering their RxD pin 3's with a grabber. Data is then transmitted from the Advantage (using control-P) as described above. Lo! The print head prints recognizable characters on the paper. After a line or two, however, the text becomes jumbled . . . the buffer has overflowed and is losing characters.

Before we pursue the handshaking matter further, let's ascertain if the Okidata has any active inputs. As before, this is accomplished by jumpering the negative voltage on the Okidata's pin 4 to the other pins on the connector. (The receiver pin 3 should not be jumpered.) If any of the Okidata's input pins is active, it will be disabled by the negative voltage and the Okidata will stop printing.

No active inputs were found on the Okidata.

We have already discovered that the Advantage's transmitter can be paused by disabling **dtr** pin 20. All that remains is to locate the pin Okidata uses to signal "buffer full" and then connect it to the Advantage's **dtr**.

Nearly all printers have front panel switches that allow the user to interrupt printing without loss of data. This switch is called ON/OFF LINE, SELECT, HOLD, READY, BUSY, or something similar. Whatever its name, the result of pushing this button is functionally the same as an overflowing buffer—the handshaking output line becomes inhibited negatively.

We'll use this SELECT switch, labeled "SEL" on the Okidata, to locate the buffer full handshaking signal. The LED tester is connected to pin 7 as usual. Then, while touching the test lead to the *active* output pins one at a time, the "SEL" switch is pushed. When the handshaking pin is reached, pushing this switch will cause the lighted LED to change from the red (positive) to the green (negative). Push it again and the red LED will illuminate again. Why do we limit our tests only to active outputs? Because we know that regardless of the particular line used for handshaking, it must either be positive or negative. Inactive pins—ones that have zero volts or ambiguous voltages—cannot possibly qualify as handshaking leads.

The first candidate for this test is the negative **RTS** pin 4. Remember, this was the handshaking pin used on our ideal printer. Wouldn't it be poetic if our very first example were to turn out to conform to that ideal model? (Sorry, **RTS** pin 4 is not it—no room for sentimentality here). Since pin 4 is not an active input, and since it does not change state for handshaking, we can safely exclude it from our cable.

The next suspect is the "unofficial" pin 11. This guess is correct. Alternately pushing the SEL switch does indeed change the LED's color back and forth. Pin 11 can now be connected to the Advantage's **dtr** pin 20. Using control-P, data is sent to the Okidata. The text begins to print, both on the screen and on paper. After a few seconds, the Okidata's buffer fills, and the display on the screen stops abruptly as the printer strives to catch up by emptying its buffer. Suddenly the screen display prints a few more lines and waits. For the duration of the printing, this hopscotch conversation between computer and printer continues. Meanwhile, the LED tester, still connected to the handshaking line, changes color in sync with the display's pauses. The interface is now working.

The final chart is shown in Figure 8.2 and Figure 8.3 shows a flowchart of the process required to locate the receiver's handshaking.

Step 5: Specify The Cable

This cable is easy to specify. Neither the Okidata nor the Advantage has any active inputs that need to be pulled up, so only three wires will be required in the cable. Figure 8.4 shows the cable.

DTE: OKIDATA 83A   DCE: NORTHSTAR ADVANTAGE

TEST RESULTS		I/O	PIN #	I/O	TEST RESULTS	
	X	!	2 TxD	?	X	
	X	?	3 RxD	!	NEG	
	NEG	!	4 RTS	!	X	
	X	?	5 CTS	!	POS	
	X	?	6 DSR	!	POS	
	X	?	8 DCD	!	POS	
HANDSHAKING	POS	–	11 —	–		
	POS	!	20 DTR	?	POS	ACTIVE

—*Figure 8.2: The Okidata/Northstar logic chart with active inputs*—

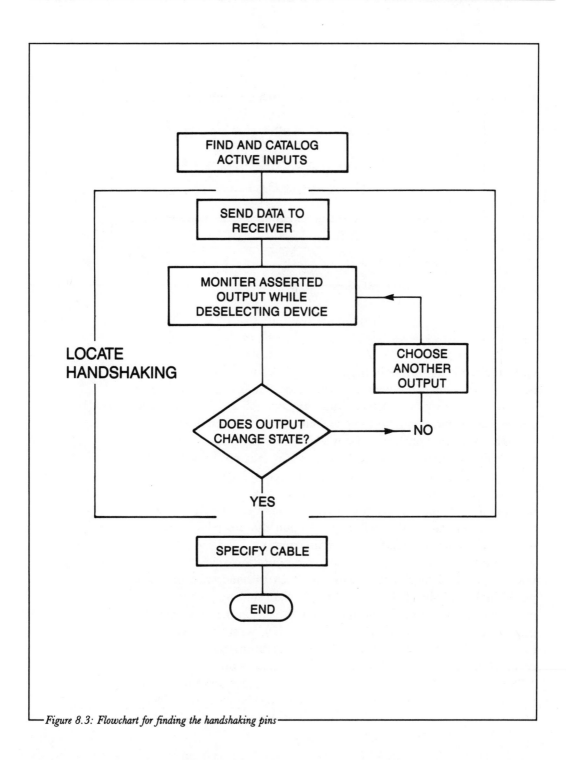

Figure 8.3: Flowchart for finding the handshaking pins

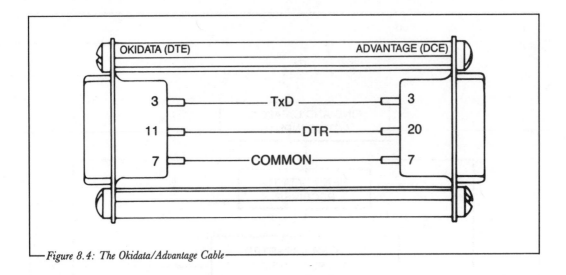

Figure 8.4: The Okidata/Advantage Cable

COMMENTS

Are you surprised to discover that we can make a "25-pin" interface work perfectly with only three wires? This simplicity is one of the best-kept secrets in computers. It is safe to say that if you are willing to sacrifice the device control logic, almost any two RS-232-C compatible devices can be interfaced on three or four wires: two data lines, handshaking, and common. As you have observed, much of the work in interfacing two serial devices is dodging the pitfalls resulting from the variable, haphazard implementation of the control logic.

In interfacing the Okidata to the Advantage, we have created a method that will permit any two devices to be interfaced. To be sure, the remaining case studies will expand upon the procedure, but the testing techniques developed will remain constant.

An examination of the Okidata documentation reveals that an internal jumper is available to allow the 83A to handshake on **DTR** pin 20 instead of pin 11. Reassignability of handshaking pins is a common feature in printers. By electing to handshake on the Okidata's **dtr** pin 20, we could have interfaced the Okidata with the Advantage using an ordinary (and expensive) 25-pin straight-through cable.

The Okidata manual also sheds light on the negative voltage on **RTS** pin 4: "Note: pins 4 and 18 may have voltages present . . . do not use." Because we have developed a custom cable, we were able to

*HOW'S THAT?
DEPARTMENT*
*. . . the cable normally
used for a receive-only
printer can be moved to
different devices as
needed, with no ill
effects.*
Data Communications for Microcomputers, *Nichols, et al,*
p. 83

ignore pin 4. Notice, however, that if the Okidata—internally jumpered to handshake on **DTR** pin 20—is connected to a DCE computer device via a 25-pin cable, the negative voltage on **RTS** pin 4 could disable the computer's **rts** input and no characters would be sent to the printer. This real possibility is yet another in a growing list of reasons *not* to use full 25-pin cables.

The Okidata documentation claims that **dsr** pin 6 on the printer is the "Signal notifying printer that data is ready to be transmitted to the printer." The meaning of this sentence remains evanescent. Furthermore, all examples of cabling in the manual show pin 6 either pulled up by jumpering to **DTR** or being enabled by a wire connected to the computer. When **dsr** pin 6 was tested, however, it was found to be inactive.

A minor complaint: the Okidata's documentation predictably claims that the printer contains an "RS-232-C interface," yet labels pin 11 **Supervisory Send Data**—a name that does not appear in the RS-232-C standard.

No harm is done with gaffes in documentation such as these. After all, who cares what pin 11 is called, or if **dsr** pin 6 is vestigial, but it does make one a bit uneasy to discover that a manufacturer doesn't understand his own product.

The Advantage's manual reveals that a jumper may be cut to enable handshaking on pin 19 instead of 20 **dtr**. The documentation also gives instructions for internally flipping the interface from DCE to DTE—a nice touch.

The Advantage's interface has one noteworthy characteristic: the handshaking input, **dtr**, has been internally pulled up. Many other computers (the KayPro, for instance) allow their handshaking lines to float open at an undefined logic level. Some of the time, an ambiguous logic state will, in fact, *disable* the handshaking input. This can present an annoyance to the user: if no printer is connected to your computer, accidentally toggling on the printer with control-P, or running an application program that performs printer output will cause the computer to *hang*, waiting for the handshaking line to be enabled. Believe it or not, there is a commercial product called "Printer Pal" ($25) that cures this problem. Yes, it's just a DB-25 connector with the handshaking line pulled up.

9

KAYPRO/EPSON CASE STUDY 3:

KAYPRO II COMPUTER (s/n 019490): CP/M portable
EPSON MX100 (s/n 349065): Dot Matrix printer with 8145 serial interface board

GENERAL CONSIDERATIONS

This may be called "The Case of The Intermittent Printer." The owner of the pair complained that her printer would operate perfectly for only a couple of pages then abruptly cease printing.

When it failed, the Epson's "offline" lamp—a lamp that monitors the printer's handshaking output—illuminated just as if the "offline" button had been pushed manually. Pushing this switch again, however, would not cause printing to proceed. The printer just froze. If the printer were switched off, then on again, it would print a few more pages before stopping. Printing a few pages at a time in this manner wasn't even an acceptable emergency solution: at power-up the printer would always return to the left margin and forget the line number it had been printing when the pause occurred.

The dealer where the owner puchased the computer was anxious to help. The printer was connected to a different brand of computer—no problem; the KayPro II was connected to a different brand of printer—no problem. It was concluded that some sort of incompatibility existed between the KayPro and the Epson. Since the woman had bought her printer mail-order after she had purchased the computer, the dealer merely pointed to a stern warning in the KayPro manual that states that the computer's manufacturer makes "no guarantees about the suitability of a given serial printer for use with the KayPro II's RS-232-C serial interface . . . before you purchase any serial printer, insist upon a demonstration of its operation." Considering the madness in the world of interfaces, this is a prudent stance for any manufacturer to take.

In the last example, you saw how the Advantage's handshaking input was internally pulled up. This allowed it, by default, to send characters to its serial port. The KayPro's handshaking pin, however, is *not* pulled up. In this case, when the initial control-P is typed, the KayPro's cursor hangs up beside the A> CP/M prompt. In this case, your *first* step will have to be to locate the computer's handshaking input. On the Advantage, the handshake input was located by applying negative voltages to the pins until a pin was found that would disable the UART and, consequently, screen output. The procedure on the KayPro is opposite: you must apply a *positive* voltage until you locate the pin that will enable the UART, causing the cursor to drop down to the next line with a new A> prompt. Once this second prompt signals that the UART's handshaking input has been enabled, printer output can be initiated as usual by typing any command that normally sends output to the screen.

This brings up an interesting point. Although the KayPro's handshaking input is not enabled by a positive pullup, neither is it disabled by a negative pulldown. In short, it is an open input and will probably behave inconsistently—disabled some of the time, enabled others. If the KayPro is used in an application that doesn't require handshaking (see the first case study in Chapter 12), its **cts** pin 5 input must be pulled up.

Step 1: Set The Baud Rate

The Epson's baud rate is set at 1200 baud by switches located on the serial board. The KayPro's baud rate is set by a utility program BAUD.COM. As with all CP/M systems, screen output is sent to the **LST:** device by typing a control-P. As delivered, the KayPro II's **LST:** device is assigned to a parallel printer. A serial printer may be assigned by typing **STAT LST: = TTY:**. If you desire the serial printer to be permanently assigned, use the utility CONFIG.COM.

Common sense suggested that the source of the problem was somehow related to the Epson's handshaking line. Surely it was not coincidental that the printer stopped working at the same time the buffer overflowed. Another clue: even though the printer's offline lamp indicated that the buffer full signal was issued, the Advantage's screen dis-

One computer consultant claims that you should never even consider buying a printer without bringing your computer into the computer store and insisting that the salesman hook everything up and make it print before you leave the store. This consultant estimates that 75% of the hardware problems people have with computers stem from a wrong cable.
InfoWorld, *June 1983*

play never broke stride. Clearly, the handshaking signal was not reaching the Advantage's UART's transmitter. To test this hypothesis, it was necessary to prevent buffer overflow altogether. How? By never sending characters to the printer faster than it can print them. If a character is printed as soon as it arrives, the buffer will never overflow. Many early serial printers (the Diablo 1610/1620, for example) were even designed to operate this way.

This is the first case where the baud rate has played an active role in interfacing, so a short discussion about baud rate is needed.

As far as we are concerned here, baud stands for "bits per second." When an 8-bit character is disassembled into individual bits for transmission, a few additional *framing bits* are inserted before and after each byte in order to delimit where one character ends and the next one begins. Thus, at least ten bits are needed to represent a single 8-bit character.

The Epson prints 80 characters per second. To assure that its buffer never overflows, we would need to send it data at a baud rate less than 80 cps times 10 bits per character or 800 baud. The nearest *lower* baud rate available is 600 baud. Better yet, 300 baud. Both the Epson and the KayPro were set to 300 baud and, as predicted, the printer performed without stalling. However, a subtle new clue was noticed: when the "Offline" button was engaged—that is, whenever the handshaking output was inhibited—the printer would pause as expected, but pushing the button would not restart the printer.

Since the owner of the Epson was anxious to utilize her printer's higher printing speed, data would have to be sent at 1200 baud. Handshaking was therefore necessary. So out with the grabbers and up with the LED tester!

As before, each input on both sides of the interface was tested for activity with a negative voltage. The results are shown in Figure 9.1. As promised, we have begun to consolidate steps.

Step 2: Ascertain The Sex Of The Equipment

Step 3: Satisfy The Control Logic

Step 4: Locate The Handshaking

There are a few new things here. First, both devices are DTEs. Flipping will not really be a problem—when the cable is designed, we can just cross 2-3, 4-5, 6-20 as necessary. Sex incompatibilites between devices has traditionally struck terror into the minds of interfacers. With the use of the logic and flowcharts, however, the physical configuration of the pins becomes unimportant—we need only figure out the requirements of both sides of the interface, then fulfill these requirements through the cable or cable adaptor.

Notice that the printer has duplicate handshaking lines. There is absolutely no difference between these two outputs. This is a good illustration of the need to include all relevant leads in every test. Once identified, of course, the transmitter and receiver need not be tested.

The Epson has two active inputs. When **dcd** pin 8 is disabled by jumpering it to a negative line (the **RTS** output on the KayPro is handy), the printer *ignores* its input data. Note that disabling this input does *not* stop the printing—instead, printing proceeds normally until all the characters in the buffer have been printed. This agrees with our UART model in Figure 3.10: special-purpose input #2 often controls the UART's receiver. Since this is not usually a useful feature, we'll need to pull up pin 8 in the cable.

The **dsr** pin 6 behaves slightly differently. If it is disabled during printing, the printing continues, the handshaking line **DTR** pin 20 becomes inhibited (negative) as usual, but doesn't become asserted again, even when the buffer empties. The handshaking signal will remain disabled until **dsr** pin 6 once again is enabled.

Unfortunately, the behavior of these pins means that you must begin each test for active inputs with an empty buffer. Unless a printer has a "CLEAR" button to flush its buffer, you will have to wait until printing stops before proceeding to test the next pin. Since the buffers

DTE: KAYPRO II   DTE: EPSON MX100

TEST RESULTS		I/O	PIN #	I/O	TEST RESULTS	
	NEG	!	2 TxD	!	NEG	
	X	?	3 RxD	?	X	
	NEG	!	4 RTS	!	X	
ACTIVE	X	?	5 CTS	?	X	
	(dimly) POS	?	6 DSR	?	X	ACTIVE
	X	?	8 DCD	?	X	ACTIVE
	X	–	11 NA	–	POS	HANDSHAKE
	POS	!	20 DTR	!	POS	HANDSHAKE

—*Figure 9.1: Logic chart for the KayPro/Epson*

on some printers hold several thousand bytes, at 1200 baud you are likely to find yourself doing a lot of waiting. For this reason, you must clear the buffer simply by turning the printer off and back on again. (If you're wondering if the Okidata from Case Study 2 had such an input, the answer is no.)

One last thing about the Epson side of the interface: there is no asserted output with which to pull up (trick) the active inputs. Accordingly, the required output must be brought over in the cable from the KayPro's **DTR** pin 20.

The KayPro's side of the interface is new, but not different. Its sole active—and therefore its handshaking—lead is **CTS** pin 5. For some reason, **RTS** pin 4 is inhibited.

Notice that the KayPro's **dsr** pin 6 is marked as "dimly POS." This means either that the output circuitry is defective or, as appears to be true here, that an internal pull up has been added.

Step 5: SPECIFY THE CABLE

Chapter 4 placed great importance upon "flipping." By now you have probably realized that flipping is just an intellectual artifice to emphasize the problems associated with same-sex interfacing. *Mental* flipping occurs as you visualize the cross-connections of complementary inputs and outputs; *physical* flipping occurs automatically when the cable is built.

The Epson side of the interface seemed a trifle elaborate, if not downright excessive, but nothing out of the ordinary. All the inputs, output, and handshaking are where they belong. Figure 9.2 shows the cable that was devised.

To everyone's delight, the printer worked perfectly with this 4-wire cable. This demonstrates that the problems were in the cable all along. An examination of the owner's cable revealed that the owner had been using a cable purchased for her by a "knowledgeable" friend. This cable supplied the connections shown in Figure 9.3.

The Epson side of the store-bought cable is a limited version of a device called a "null modem." A null cable is really a cable of tricks designed to trick an RS-232-C conforming device into passing data. Notice that only the data lines (pins 2 and 3) and the COMMON are connected from one side of the interface to the other. The **RTS** pin 4 output is "wrapped around" to enable the **cts** pin 5 input *and* the **dcd** pin 8 input. Similarly, **DTR** pin 20, an output on a strict RS-232-C device, is used to enable its complementary input, **dsr** pin 6. The complementary action occurs on the DCE side. Sounds like a useful gadget, doesn't it? Well, the catch is that unless the pin assignments adhere to the standard RS-232-C standard, strange things occur. Even if a handshaking signal had been installed in this null modem cable, it would have been eaten by being connected to another asserted output. Since the RS-232-C interface standard doesn't support handshaking per se, off-the-shelf null modems are usually of little use with microcomputers in general, and especially with printers or other devices that require a controlled flow of data.

The cable itself showed evidence of a great struggle. Many of the connectors were loose from having been overheated, the wires' insulation was charred and peeled away, and most of the pins had telltale short wire stubs left over from failed experiments with jumpers. While this cable began life as an off-the-shelf null cable, the knowledgeable friend soon discovered that the printer wouldn't function at all with it.

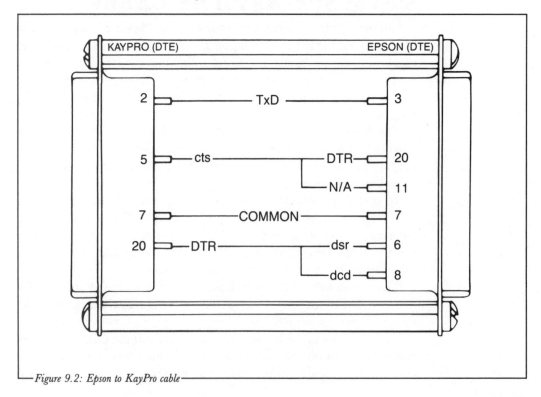

Figure 9.2: Epson to KayPro cable

The friend then began furiously to rewire the cable by adding and removing jumpers, then soldering new wires. After several hours, the friend declared the printer to be working. Indeed, it printed a page or so nicely, but no one thought to test the printer over a longer period of four or five pages.

Notice that the pullup between the KayPro's RTS and **cts** had been cut, and that **DTR** was used to pull up all three inputs **cts**, **dsr**, and **dcd**. Can you see why the printer would not work at all with the full null cable? The null cable assumes that **RTS** will be asserted and will therefore enable **cts**. But on the KayPro, **RST** is *inhibited*, which disables the handshaking input.

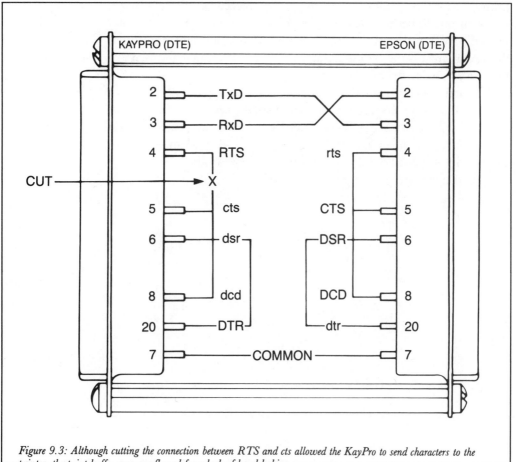

Figure 9.3: Although cutting the connection between RTS and cts allowed the KayPro to send characters to the printer, the print buffer soon overflowed from lack of handshaking.

The mere absence of handshaking in this cable, of course, would have prevented normal printer operation. The Epson's 2,000 character print buffer will easily store a single page of text. But a large buffer is not a viable substitute for handshaking—it just postpones the inevitable. Since the KayPro could not have received the Epson's "buffer full" signal, the contents of the buffer would sooner or later have been overwritten by new incoming characters. But have you figured out why printing stopped when the Epson's handshaking line, **DTR** pin 20, was inhibited? Notice that the handshaking line is jumpered to an active input, **dsr** pin 6. We previously discovered that, when disabled, **dsr** pin 6 causes the printer to withhold its handshaking signal. In addition, a disabled **dcd** pin 8 prevented new incoming characters from reaching the buffer. When the buffer overflows, the handshake signal on pin 20 became negative, disabling both inputs **dcd** pin 8 and **dsr** pin 6. When the remaining characters in the buffer were printed, the Epson froze—the handshaking line could not signal the KayPro for another buffer full of characters.

This action of one logic state initiating a second logic state which, in turn, reinforces the first logic state, is known as *latching,* or, more metaphorically, a *deadly embrace.* When interconnected, **dtr** pin 6 and *any* handshaking pin form such a latch. So, the null modem—a useful device on a standard RS-232-C implementation—in this case actually prevented the printer from operating correctly.

OSBORNE/VOTRAX CASE STUDY 4:

10

OSBORNE I (SN007353): portable CP/M computer.
VOTRAX TYPE 'N TALK (SN00089): speech
enunciator.

GENERAL CONSIDERATIONS

The Type 'n Talk is an amusing device. When fed a stream of serial characters, it attempts to convert them to English words or sounds, then announces them with a helium-Scandinavian intonation.

The Type 'n Talk appears to have strewn the bodies of a great number of interfacers in its wake. Their interfacing tales included garbled sounds, omitted text, hanging up after a few words (like the Epson in Case Study 3), and outright refusal to make a sound. The most astounding allegation against Type 'n Talk was that it mumbled—a charge never confirmed. At any rate, any device with such a bad reputation deserves to be tamed in print.

Step 1: Set The Baud Rate

The Osborne's baud rate is set by microswitches inside the computer. The Type 'n Talk is set with switches on the back panel. Both devices were set for 1200 baud.

The Osborne's serial port was assigned to the physical device name **CRT:**. To use a serial printer, execute the CP/M command **STAT LST: = CRT:**. As with any CP/M system, screen output can then be sent to the **LST:** device with control-P.

Aside from the novelty of speaking, the Type 'n Talk is just another serial device in search of handshaking. While awaiting enunciation, characters are stored in a modestly-sized buffer whose overflow is signaled by the inhibition of a pin on the RS-232-C interface. In order

for Type 'n Talk's speech to be intelligible, it must speak slowly, so
that even the slowest baud rate is likely to cause buffer overflow. We
set it for 1200 because we want the buffer to overflow quickly in order
to expedite testing.

Step 2: Ascertain The Sex of The Devices

Step 3: Satisfy The Control Logic

The full interface chart is shown in Figure 10.1. At first glance, this
looks like a felicitous marriage. Nothing could be more vanilla than
the Osborne side of the interface: a single active input, **dtr** pin 20 with
two asserted outputs to use for tricks and pullups. Like the Advantage,
the Osborne's handshaking line is pulled up. The Type 'n Talk looks
simple at first, too. **TxD** pin 2 is negative—a DTE, right? **DTR** pin 20
is an asserted output—a DTE, right? **CTS** pin 5 an asserted output—a
DTE, wrong. **CTS** pin 5 is not supposed to be a DTE output—it's an
input. Well, maybe the manufacturer has installed an internal pullup
to assure its logic state. Perhaps, but if **CTS** is a pulled-up input, it
should be active, or why go to the trouble? But our logic chart shows
that it isn't active. Moreover, if **CTS** pin 5 is an input, it is likely
that **RTS** pin 4, its complement, would be asserted; but the Type 'n
Talk's **RTS** pin 4 is not an output—it is neither positive nor negative.

Step 4: Locate The Handshaking

When in doubt about how to proceed, always try the device with
data alone—no logic control or handshaking. Frequently this will

DTE: VOTRAX TYPE 'N TALK   DCE: OSBORNE I

TEST RESULTS	I/O	PIN #	I/O	TEST RESULTS	
NEG	!	2 TxD	?	X	
X	?	3 RxD	!	NEG	
X	!	4 RTS	?	X	
POS	?	5 CTS	!	POS	
X	?	6 DSR	!	POS	
X	?	8 DCD	!	X	
POS	!	20 DTR	?	POS	ACTIVE

Figure 10.1: Logic chart for Osborne/Type 'n Talk

reveal behavior that you can make sense of. In this case, however, the Type 'n Talk uttered not a peep.

Next we can try a limited null modem cable explained in Case Study 3. The **RTS** pin 4 and **CTS** pin 5 pair are connected. Similarly, the output of **DTR** pin 20 is used to assert the inputs **dsr** pin 6 and **dcd** pin 8. Any DTE interface that won't respond *somehow* to this treatment doesn't have much claim to RS-232-C compatibility.

Tediously, Type 'n Talk began to read the text of the Wordstar demo file EXAMPLE.TXT. But after only a few words, it stopped. Usually, when we succeed in getting the data to flow, we immediately test for active inputs, but only when the data will flow continuously. Don't make the test for active inputs until you have figured out why a device hangs up and stops working. As soon as the hangup occurs, measure the pins again...something must have changed to cause the data flow to stop!

Testing the Type 'n Talk's pins again revealed that the jumpered pins **RTS** pin 4 and **CTS** pin 5 have both become negative! "Aha," you say, "**CTS** pin 5 is a pulled up input." On the contrary, when the jumper between these pins is removed, it is pin 5 **CTS** that has changed state. So the buffer full signal occurs on **CTS** pin 5—normally a DTE input. When **CTS** pin 5 became negative, the negative voltage was applied to **RTS** pin 4 via the jumper wire. Because it effectively stopped the transfer of data to the Type 'n Talk's buffer, **RTS** pin 4— normally an output—must therefore be an active input.

After discovery of this unusual arrangement, pin 4 (it can't really be called a DTE input **rts**, can it?) could be enabled by tricking it to **DTR** pin 20. This enabled the continuous flow of data between the Osborne and the Type 'n Talk. Normal testing revealed that **dcd** pin 8 was an active input that caused the Type 'n Talk (like the Epson) to ignore incoming data. When **dcd** pin 8 was disabled, Type 'n Talk would talk out the words remaining in its buffer, then fall into silence. The disabled **dcd** would not allow any more characters into the buffer. This behavior, you will recall, is predicted by our UART model: **dcd** is generally a special-purpose input used to switch the receiver on and off.

Pin 4 functioned in a different, but complementary fashion. After pin 4 was disabled, the Type 'n Talk would work normally until its handshaking line (pin 5) signaled a full buffer by becoming negative; after this, the handshaking line never became asserted again. When the current buffer was exhausted, no request for additional characters was made.

Figure 10.2 shows the final chart on the interface.

Step 5: Specify The Cable

Considering the grief the Type 'n Talk has caused, the cable shown in Figure 10.3 is a simple one. The Type 'n Talk handshake line, pin

DTE: VOTRAX TYPE 'N TALK   DCE: OSBORNE I

TEST RESULTS		I/O	PIN #	I/O	TEST RESULTS	
	NEG	!	2 TxD	?	X	
	X	?	3 RxD	!	NEG	
	X	?	4 xxx	?	X	
HANDSHAKING	POS	1	5 xxx	!	POS	
	X	?	6 DSR	!	POS	
	X	?	8 DCD	!	X	
	POS	!	20 DTR	?	POS	ACTIVE

—Figure 10.2—

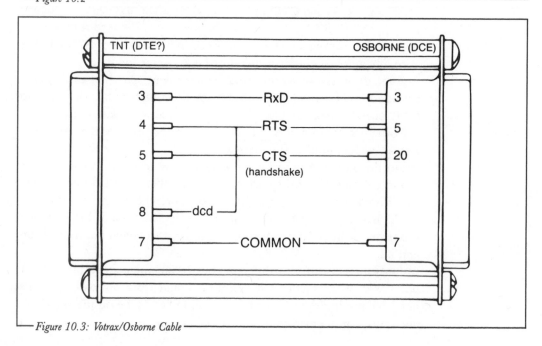

— Figure 10.3: Votrax/Osborne Cable —

5, is connected to the only Osborne active input, **DTR** pin 20. The Type 'n Talk has been known to make extremely rude noises at power up and power down. Since the Osborne's **CTS** pin 5 is asserted only when its power is on, this pin is used to disable the two active inputs. Data exchange occurs between the pin 3's as usual.

COMMENTS

If this sounds like the KayPro/Epson case study, it is only because the same phenomenon, self-latching, was the clue in both cases. The similarity ends there, however. Nothing was wrong with the Epson—it had simply been incorrectly cabled. The Type 'n Talk, on the other hand, has a confusing pin assignment. In view of this arbitrary rearrangement of pins, it is no surprise the Type 'n Talk has the reputation of causing interfacing ulcers.

One is tempted to conclude that the unit is miswired. But this theory contradicts the manufacturer's manual, which explicitly names pin 4 as **RTS** and pin 5 as **CTS**. Type 'n Talk is not miswired, nor is the manual in error. It is just another example of a willy-nilly implementation of RS-232-C "compatibility."

The Osborne manual implies that **RTS** pin 4 is active, and the Type 'n Talk manual implies that its pin 6 is active. Neither manual proved to be correct. Don't be surprised to discover that interfaces don't always behave as advertised. Frequently a manufacturer will make "noncritical" changes in their circuitry, but neglect to document them in their manuals.

You may wonder why Type 'n Talk has a transmitter. Several of these devices can be daisy-chained into a kind of network, each unit passing information (codes) to the next unit down the chain. Although it is hard to imagine when this feature might be useful, it does pose some bizarre interfacing possibilities.

11

IBM/NEC
CASE STUDY 5:

IBM PERSONAL COMPUTER (SN271283):
integrated computer with PC DOS operating system.
NEC SPINWRITER 3510 (SN541510417):
35 cps letter-quality serial printer.

GENERAL CONSIDERATIONS

Although this case study illustrates some interesting points, it has another reason for being included: letter-quality printers are supposed to be difficult to interface. As a matter of fact, when this Spinwriter was rented from a local rental agency, the agent warned that it could not be interfaced with the IBM PC. The prevalence of this sort of thinking defies explanation. The KayPro/Epson combo was diagnosed as incompatible because each would work satisfactorily with other units. The term "incompatible" is used, one suspects, as a euphemism for "a problem we can't figure out." You should take it as a matter of Euclidian faith that if two RS-232-C devices can be interfaced to other RS-232-C devices, they can be interfaced to each other.

The PC/Spinwriter under study would print absolutely nothing.

Step 1: Set The Baud Rate

The PC's baud rate is set with the PC DOS command, **MODE COM1:1200,N,8,1,P**. The RS-232-C port can be assigned to PC DOS's equivalent of CP/M's **LST:** device by typing: **MODE LPT1: = COM1:**. You can make these settings *permanent* by installing the

MODE command above in the automatic login file, **AUTOEXEC.BAT**. The command will then be automatically executed each time you power on the PC.

In addition to toggling the printer with control-P as in CP/M, the contents of the PC's screen can be sent to the printer by typing (SHIFT)-PRTSC (print screen). Otherwise, the behavior and the testing procedure is the same as with other examples.

The Spinwriter's baud rate is set by means of small switches on the front panel.

The owners of this equipment planned to use it with the popular word processing program, WordStar. WordStar permits a file to be printed "in the background" while another document is being edited. During the time the computer is actually sending characters to the printer, however, the computer cannot simultaneously fetch incoming characters typed on the keyboard. In order to minimize this "dropped character" problem, the transfer between computer and printer should take place at the highest possible baud rate.

We selected the highest speed at which both the PC and the Spinwriter will operate: 9600 baud.

Step 2: Ascertain The Sex Of The Equipment

Step 3: Satisfy The Control Logic

Step 4: Locate The Handshaking

Notice that we have now consolidated three steps into one. By now you are aware that, in actual practice, these three steps are accomplished simultaneously. This consolidation will continue until, in Chapter 12 (Interfacing Modems), the steps disappear entirely. By the time you finish that chapter, you will perceive interfacing not so much as a series of steps than as an inductive *process*.

Measuring each pin with the LED tester produced the interface chart shown in Figure 11.1.

This is the busiest interface we have seen so far. Pins below the dotted line represent inhibited outputs: the Spinwriter's pins 23 and 25 are used for *auxiliary* signals such as "out of paper." It is left to curiosity to investigate these pins on your own. Suffice it to say that they do not affect the basic interfacing of the Spinwriter to a computer.

Notice that the Spinwriter implements our entire subset of DTE logic control (i.e., the BIG EIGHT). This is quite common for letter-quality printers. Printers such as the Spinwriter came to microcomputers by way of the world of the mainframe and minicomputer where printers are frequently used as *remote* printout devices. For example, a company with many offices, each requiring printed copy, would transmit information by telephone (with modems on each end) from the main computer to a printer on the other end. Since all modems once came directly from the telephone company, all devices that were intended to interface to modems had to comply with the official RS-232-C interface standard. Although seldom used, this true modem compatibility has been handed down to microcomputer users. Ironically, it is this faithful implementation of the genuine RS-232-C interface standard that gives these printers their reputation for obstinance.

Do you see the glaring anomaly on the Spinwriter side? Its handshaking line, pin 19, is *inhibited*. When applied to the PC's handshaking input **rts** pin 5, this negative voltage disables the PC UART's transmitter. In short, the Spinwriter is signaling "OK to transmit" with a signal that the PC interprets as "do not transmit."

Somewhere there is a piece of equipment—whose identity has so far eluded discovery—that responds to an inverted handshaking signal. The inverted handshaking output on the Spinwriter's pin 19 was easily corrected: through the use of internal switches or jumpers, virtually all printers today have the ability to change the polarity of the

DTE: NEC SPINWRITER   DTE: IBM PC

TEST RESULTS		I/O	PIN #	I/O	TEST RESULTS	
	NEG	!	2 TxD	!	NEG	
	X	?	3 RxD	?	X	
	POS	!	4 RTS	!	POS	
ACTIVE	X	?	5 CTS	?	X	ACTIVE
ACTIVE	X	?	6 DSR	?	X	ACTIVE
ACTIVE	X	?	8 DCD	?	X	
HANDSHAKING	NEG	–	19 —	–	X	
	POS	!	20 DTR	!	POS	
	NEG	–	23 N/A	–	X	
	NEG	–	25 N/A	–	X	

—*Figure 11.1: Logic Chart for spinwriter and IBM PC*

handshake signal. Many also have the ability to reassign the pins on which the handshaking signal will occur.

The IBM side looks like business as usual. The only odd thing is that there is apparently no difference between the behavior of **cts** pin 5 and **dsr** pin 6—either will pause the UART's transmitter, and both are internally pulled up.

Although the **dcd** inputs have not been listed as "ACTIVE" on the computers' logic charts, this does not tell the whole story. The primary function of **dcd** pin 8 is to pause the UART's receiver. When driving a printer, however, a computer receives no data from a printer (unless software handshaking is performed). In other words, we have no way of knowing if **dcd** will pause the receiver or not. The purpose of this warning is merely to alert you that every different application—software handshaking, for example—may require a different cable. A modem/terminal program, for example, will need to send as well as receive characters, in which case it may be necessary to pull up **dcd** pin 8. The chart and cable derived for a particular device, therefore, reflect only the immediate interfacing requirements for that device. The same device in another application may require an entirely different cable.

Step 5: Specify The Cable

On a particularly active interface, one is often tempted to construct a cable by running complementary pairs from one side of the interface to the other. Here for example, we might be tempted to use the **DTR** pin 20 on each side of the interface to enable the **dsr** on the other. Likewise we might want to use the asserted **RTS** pin 4 on the IBM side to enable the active input of **cts** pin 5 on the Spinwriter.

Aside from satisfying a desire for symmetry, exactly what would be accomplished by running all these wires? Unless you are implementing a full modem control interface, these wires will accomplish nothing useful. The frequency of failure of a cable is proportional to the number of its wires. If wires accomplish nothing, they should be omitted. Whenever possible, use tricks and pullups from the local interface instead of bringing them over by cable.

The recommended cable is shown in Figure 11.2.

Like many printers, the Spinwriter contains microswitches to pull up its active inputs, in this case **cts** pin 5, **dsr** pin 6, **dcd** pin 8. By using these switches, the cable in Figure 11.3 would have been serviceable, though not recommended.

Why opt for a more complicated cable when a simple one will do? It is good practice to make your cables accommodate any possible configuration of the equipment. The recommended cable, for example, will work with any PC/Spinwriter, regardless of the trick switch settings, but the simpler cable will work only if these switches are engaged. Because it is more general, the recommended cable is a better design.

COMMENTS

This particular IBM PC behaved irregularly during testing. Normally, any negative output may be employed in locating the active inputs. On this sample, however, the negative **TxD** output pin 2 would not consistently pause the IBM's transmitter once the data flow was *in progress* although it would successfully prevent transmission if connected *before* activating the PRTSC key.

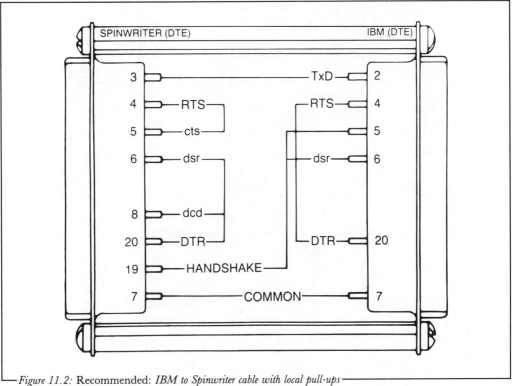

Figure 11.2: Recommended: *IBM to Spinwriter cable with local pull-ups*

Although other samples of the PC have since been tested as usual without difficulty, this problem did cause considerable head-scratching for a while. The problem was solved by using a 9 volt transistor battery as the source for the negative voltage. Figure 11.4 shows how the

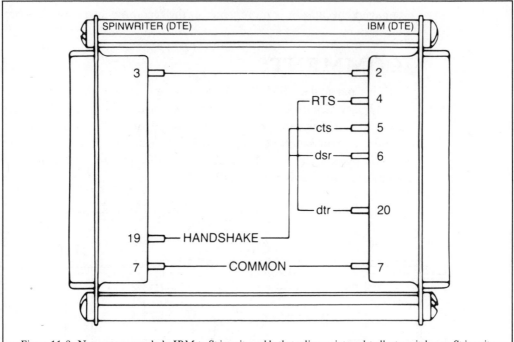

Figure 11.3: Not recommended: *IBM to Spinwriter cable that relies on internal pull-up switches on Spinwriter*

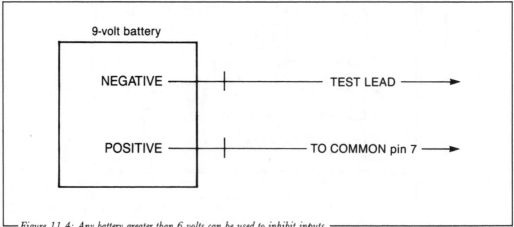

Figure 11.4: Any battery greater than 6 volts can be used to inhibit inputs.

HOW'S THAT?
DEPARTMENT

Now, I had seen my word processor hang before with another printer, and I had discovered the problem to be a missing "request to send" signal on pin 4 of the RS-232-C connector. Could the Daisywriter's interface cable have the same problem?

Sure enough—the interface cable only supplied signals to eight of the 25 pins of the connector. And pin 4 was not one of the eight. A telephone inquiry to the distributor solved the mystery—but not the problem. My interface is an earlier version than the one his cable guide listed. So for the cost of $50, I was granted the opportunity to rebuild my cable.

This is the weakest link in the installation of the Daisywriter. It is absolutely critical that you give your dealer the model and serial number of the interface you'll be using. I expect, however, that Computers International should have supplied signals to all the pins specified in the RS-232-C standard.
InfoWorld, *June 13, 1983*

battery was connected. As usual, all connections were made with grabbers.

As shown, the positive (+) terminal of the battery is connected to COMMON pin 7. The other lead is connected to the battery's negative (−) terminal and becomes the TEST lead used to test for active inputs. The battery can, of course, be substituted for an asserted output if you should encounter a device with no outputs asserted. To substitute the battery for a positive source, connect the negative battery terminal to COMMON pin 7 on the interface.

CONCLUSION

We have studied a series of typical and not so typical interface cases and problems. Notice that every one of the interfaces has been achieved with *four wires or fewer* across the interface. Practically everyone is astounded to discover the basic simplicity of the final cabling. Don't forget, one of the great advantages a serial interface has over a parallel one is the reduced aggravation of wiring. A parallel interface can be achieved with as few as nine wires. Although there are other advantages to serial data transmission, the more wires you use, the more your serial interface will look parallel.

The method of construction of a final cable is largely a matter of personal taste and temperament. For those who decline to solder, solderless connectors will be the method of choice. If you need to interface only one device, certainly a custom cable for your application is indicated. But if you have a large computer installation with several printers and modems, if your business uses computers in more than one office, or if you just like to play with new toys, you will soon find yourself entangled in a thicket of unique cables.

To avoid this proliferation of wires, you may choose not to make cables at all, but to use the test adaptor as a *cable header* instead. Once you have achieved a satisfactory interface on the test adaptor, permanently solder the appropriate wires into place, then install it on the correct end of the cable. Construct a good supply of identical cables, using a subgroup of frequently-used wires. Cables with 11 wires— 2,3,4,5,6,7,8,11,19,20,21—will satisfy 99 percent of your requirements. With this technique, all your cables are interchangeable; only the adaptor will be unique. The adaptor can be easily modified, repaired, or completely rewired for a new application. Best of all, you will find it easier to manage a pile of obvious adaptors than a nightmare of cables of dubious configuration.

The convenience attained by the use of adaptors in place of hardwired cables does not come for free: there is no secure way to affix the adaptor to the equipment. The friction fit between connectors will hold the adaptor firmly in place, but can become unplugged when the equipment is moved or when the cable is tugged.

We have now accomplished our stated goal—how to decode the control and handshaking logic, then connect the wires that carry data from one serial device to another.

There may appear to be a glaring omission in our case studies—no modems. This topic will be left for exclusive treatment in the next chapter.

In Figure 11.5 you will see the final flowchart.

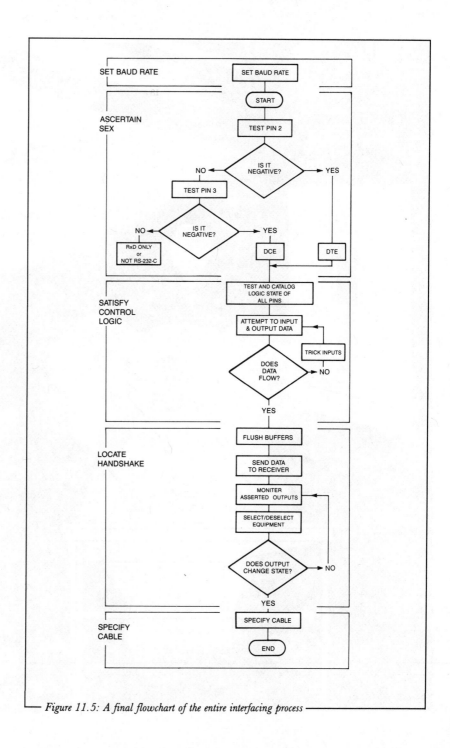

Figure 11.5: A final flowchart of the entire interfacing process

12

INTERFACING MODEMS

At first it may seem queer to arrive at the subject of modem interfacing by way of examples of aberrant implementations of the RS-232-C standard. Traditional discussions of this subject begin with an explanation of how modems work, follow with a detailed exegesis of modem control as documented in the RS-232-C standard, and finish up with examples of deviations from the standard. That this approach has failed to produce a single piece of intelligible literature bespeaks a need for an alternative treatment.

Upon further reflection, our apparently circuitous path to the topic of modem interfacing is a perfectly sensible one. This book, after all, isn't about modems, but about interfacing "RS-232-C compatible" devices to microcomputers. Only a small fraction of these devices are modems. Moreover, only a few of the formal modem control mechanisms described in the RS-232-C standard are actually found on microcomputers. In other words, the RS-232-C standard is no more or less relevant to interfacing modems and microcomputers than it is to printers and terminals.

The modems designed for microcomputers bear little resemblance to those for which the RS-232-C standard was written. Until recently, microcomputer owners interested in telecommunications had to settle for Bell-style modems. Since there were few microcomputers, the modem market was dominated by units intended for use in the world of large computers. These "data sets," as Bell calls them, had to conform rigorously to the RS-232-C standard. Casual or hobbyist users therefore had to purchase equipment whose complexity increased not only its cost but also the aggravation associated with interfacing.

As the number of micros grew, the "finer" points of the RS-232-C standard were ignored. Modem manufacturers began to design equipment for their simpler, UART-based interfaces and the modest requirements of micros. Strictly speaking, it is now scarcely possible to implement the full complement of RS-232-C modem controls with the UARTs used in micros today. Recall that a full-blown DTE interface employs three control inputs (**cts**, **dsr**, and **dcd**). But the UARTs in our test microcomputers offer only two inputs. So we couldn't fully implement an interface, even if we wanted to. While it is possible to monitor additional inputs and outputs by dedicating additional circuitry to the task, such hardware refinements are usually offered only as part of expensive "professional communications" options.

In summary, the modem interfaces designed for microcomputers reflect the characteristics of the micro and not the official device control logic of the RS-232-C standard. But if for no other reason than historical curiosity, modems deserve a special treatment among a host of other, equally interesting equipment.

A MODEM PRIMER: PULLING THE LION'S TAIL

For incomprehensible reasons, the microcomputer user tends to view modems with a mixture of awe and reverence. Yet modems are less complex than almost any other type of peripheral. A peek inside even the most basic printer reveals considerable circuitry. By comparison, modems are simple—the basic 300 baud modem is even available as a single integrated circuit. (This almost guarantees that it will take its place beside the UART as a service device. It is a safe wager that every computer will soon include a modem among its *built-in* hardware.)

The telephone system was designed for one purpose only: human voice communications. Speech can be recognizably reproduced with an amazingly narrow band of audio frequencies, from 500 Hz to 1000 Hz. Although public telephone lines (officially, "switched telephone networks") will reproduce all tones in the range 300-3300 Hz, certain other "signaling tones" in this range prohibit the transmission of

It is generally claimed that the word "modem" is a portmanteau word derived from the technical terms MODulation (the process of converting bits into tones) and DEModulation (the process of converting the tones back to bits). In fact, the term may be a corruption of the name of the Gaelic warrior hero, Mordem, who reportedly used lions to send code during battle. As reported by the eighteenth century historian James Macpherson, lions with distinctive roars were chosen in pairs. Code was generated by pulling the appropriate lion's tail, one tail for dots and the other for dashes. It is conjectured that the success of this practice explains the great number of lions found on heraldic coats of arms. At any rate, the parallel between this ancient practice and modem technology is, you must agree, uncanny.

continuous tones above about 2400 Hz. This leaves the phone with a usable frequency range of 300-2400 Hz, grossly inadequate for the undistorted reproduction of fast-moving serial bit-pulses. Successful transmission of binary data pulses would require the telephone to be able to reproduce all frequencies from 0 to 300 kiloHertz, far beyond the capabilities of even the most sophisticated high-fidelity components, much less the telephone equipment.

The problem then becomes how to convert these electrical bit-pulses into audio tones reproducible by telephone equipment. Luckily, this problem has a simple solution: convert the data pulses to audible tones, send them down the telephone lines like any other sound, then convert them back to data on the other end. A modem accomplishes these feats by means of two audio tone generators. When the modem receives a binary 1 (MARK) through its RS-232-C interface, it sends one of the tones down the phone lines for the duration of that bit. In an identical manner, the other tone generator is activated when 0 (SPACE) is received. These tones, once injected into the phone lines, are thereafter treated no differently than ordinary speech.

On the receiving end, the modem listens to the telephone lines. When the higher frequency tone arrives, the modem transmits a 1 from its RS-232-C interface; when the other tone is received, the modem translates it into 0 for the interface. In this manner, the bit patterns translated on one end are recovered exactly on the other.

Notice that this scheme, known as the *simplex* mode, permits communication only in one direction. In *half-duplex* operation, the circuitry on the modems on both ends are *alternately* switched between transmitting and receiving. Half-duplex is analogous to CB radio, where either end may send or receive, but not both simultaneously. The radio operator changes the equipment from receive to transmit by pushing a button on the microphone. When the transmission is complete, the talker signals the end of transmission by using the word "over" (a kind of "software" handshaking, if you will). This familiar set of protocols is close to those used in half-duplex modem operation. Normally, computer/modem A is in transmit while computer/modem B is in receive mode. At the end of its message, A appends a predetermined code to its data stream (like the "over" in the radio transmission) to inform B that transmission is now complete.

Immediately after sending this "end of message" code, system A must prepare for receiving. As the first step in switching to the receive mode, the computer inhibits its **REQUEST TO SEND** line. The modem interprets the absence of this signal as a request to receive. The switch-over from transmit to receive (or vice versa) is referred to as "turning the line around," and takes a few milliseconds. When modem A has made the necessary internal circuitry changes, it inhibits its **CLEAR TO SEND** output to indicate that it is ready to receive.

Meanwhile, at the B end, a parallel but opposite set of events is occurring in preparation for transmission. Upon receipt of the imbedded "over" code, the B computer asserts **RTS** to force its modem to switch its receiver circuitry to the transmit mode. When the switch-over is complete the modem asserts **CTS** to inform the computer that it is now ready to act as a transmitter.

The Two-Tone Communications Link

Simultaneous bidirectional data transfer, *full-duplex*, is effected by adopting yet another, different pair of tones for the opposite direction. This obviates the half-duplex process of turning the line around. For example, a 300 baud full-duplex modem represents a 1 with a 1270 Hz tone and a 0 with a tone of 1070 Hz. Thus, at any moment, one modem is transmitting data with 1070/1270 Hz tones to another modem that is listening for these tones. At the same time, an identical action is occurring in the other direction with the tone-pair 2025/2225 Hz. The tone-pair assignment for *full-duplex communication scheme* is shown for 300 baud in Figure 12.1.

Unless both ends agree which tone-pair will be used for which direction, a conflict may exist. Obviously no communication could take place, for example, if one end were transmitting on 1070/1270 Hz, while the other were listening for 2025/2225 Hz. This problem is

A small point of clarification: it has been widely and incorrectly reported that all modems transmit a special carrier tone in order to broadcast their presence on the line. But because an idling RS-232-C line by definition generates a MARK, 300 baud modems do not issue "carrier" tones. This misconception is doubtless perpetuated by the use of the apocryphal name DATA CARRIER DETECT to stand for RECEIVED LINE SIGNAL DETECT. With Bell 212-type 1200 baud modems, which encode 1's and 0's differently from 300 baud, there is a more legitimate reason to use the term "carrier." Here logic levels are represented not as discrete tones, but as phase changes in a tone of constant frequency. A discussion of modem modulation techniques is not within the scope of this book, but, if you have a 212A. type

ORIGINATE		ANSWER	
1	0	1	0
1270	1070	2225	2025

Figure 12.1: 300 baud frequency assignments for Bell "compatible" (North American) modems.

modem, you can perform an experiment to demonstrate how 1200 baud operation fundamentally differs from 300 baud. First establish a data link at 300 baud. Listen in on the telephone line as you type characters. With each character, you will hear a shift in tones on the phone line. Now establish a data link at 1200 baud and type some characters. Now the tones on the telephone lines do not change.

nicely solved by adopting a convention: when a modem originates a call, it transmits on 1070/1270 Hz and receives on 2025/2225 Hz. The modem is placed in *originate* or answer mode either by means of a switch, or, in the case of auto-answer modems, by circuitry activated by an incoming call. A modem that answers a call uses the complementary assignments, sending on 2025/2225 Hz while receiving on 1070/1270 Hz.

When the modem is first connected to the phone line, it will be generating the higher of its two tones, a logical 1. Why a 1? Remember that an *idle* RS-232-C transmitter will always produce a negative voltage which, in the inverted logic of the RS-232-C standard, is a logical 1 (MARK). A MARK causes the modem to idle at the higher frequency. When the answering modem recognizes this incoming MARK tone, it responds by sending its own assigned MARK tone down the telephone line. When both ends have received tones of the expected frequency, the data connection—sometimes called a *data link*—is complete and communication may begin.

When one modem sees an incoming idle-state tone, it responds by asserting its **DCD** output. Some DTE's use this signal—along with **DSR**—as a precondition for *any* kind of communication; it is the DTE's way of knowing that another modem is on the other end, ready to talk.

It is interesting to note that since it doesn't have to reverse its transmitter and receiver, full-duplex modem control does not require the use of **RTS** and **CTS**. These leads are nevertheless frequently found on microcomputers.

Bell Compatibility

There's that word again: "compatibility." Its meaning is no more concrete than when used in "RS-232-C compatible." Many of the features of Bell equipment are not included in this compatibility. For example, the most common modem is the Bell 103 modem, a 300 baud, full-duplex originate/answer modem. Virtually every modem manufacturer makes a product claiming compatibility with the Bell 103. The Bell version has some interesting features, including automatic disconnection from the telephone line when the link is broken (as when the other end hangs up), and the ability to be switched between originate and answer state by software. It is unlikely that microcomputer modems in the $100–$200 range will offer interchangeability in these areas. So, after the fog of advertising hyperbole has cleared, Bell compatibility really just means that the modem in question uses the same frequencies as its Bell counterpart.

Many of the Bell models are intended for exotic (for micro users, anyway) applications, such as use on leased lines at 9600 baud. As a practical matter, then, only a few Bell models are suitable for micro use. The chart in Figure 12.2 is a brief summary of the characteristics of important Bell models.

PRACTICAL MODEM INTERFACING

When we try to apply our usual testing procedures to modems, two problems immediately confront us. The first problem is caused by an inadequacy in most microcomputer operating systems. You have seen that an operating system provides handy ways to utilize its resources: characters typed at a keyboard are automatically displayed on a video screen; characters can be sent to a printer with the push of a key. Unfortunately, no such support exists for modems. As modems become a built-in commodity in computers, however, operating systems will begin to accommodate them. Just as we can toggle our

COMMUNICATIONS PARAMETERS	MANUAL ORIG ONLY	MANUAL ANSWER ONLY	MANUAL ORIG/ANSWER	AUTOMATIC ANSWER
300 BAUD FULL DUPLEX	113A 113C	113D	103A 103J 212A	103A 103J 113B 113D 212A
1200 BAUD HALF-DUPLEX			202S	202S
1200 BAUD FULL-DUPLEX			212	212
300/1200 BAUD FULL-DUPLEX			212A	212A

Figure 12.2: Summary of characteristics of important Bell modems

printer in CP/M with a simple control-P, so future operating systems will allow us to send keyboard output to and derive input from modems. With modems thus considered an "environmental" resource like printers, terminals, and disk drives, modem application programs (indeed, general-purpose serial I/O) will be written that will run without customization for each computer.

When interfacing a modem to a terminal, the means exists to generate characters for modem transmission and to display the characters received by your modem. However, application software is necessary if you are interfacing a modem to a microcomputer. This software, called a *terminal emulator*, administrates the triad of keyboard-modem-CRT just as if they were a terminal. Assuming that you have the correct software in hand (or are interfacing a terminal), a second problem arises because the operation of a correctly interfaced modem is essentially transparent. Unlike the printer that gives immediate response by printing characters on paper, a modem doesn't give any direct evidence that it is working. Aside from reduced speed, and perhaps an occasional strange character caused by a noise *glitch* on the phone line, the user is never even aware of a modem when interfaced correctly. When a character is sent to the modem, it is promptly converted to an audio tone, then injected into the telephone line. Incoming characters arriving as audio tones are converted to a serial bit stream and transmitted to the computer by the modem's RS-232-C interface. With the addition of certain optional features, a modem will act *both* as data source and destination.

Optional Modem Features

When the normal fate of characters is to disappear unheralded onto the phone line, what sign do we have that the modem is working at all? Likewise, where can we obtain the incoming signals with which to test the modem's receiving functions?

Three optional features are important to modem interfacing specifically and to modem use in general. The most basic of these features are indicator lamps to monitor the state of certain pins on its RS-232-C connector: **txd**, **RxD**, **DSR**, and **DCD** are the most useful. Each time an outbound character is received at the modem's receiver, the lamp representing pin 2 will flash. A different lamp is activated by outbound characters. During interfacing, or later when the whole system suddenly and inexplicably stops working, these flashing lights will be an important source of diagnostic information.

Another valuable feature is the automatic *echo* of characters. If the modem is not in a data link, any character arriving at **rxd** pin 2 is immediately looped back and transmitted on **RxD** pin 3. This feature, combined with the monitor feature just described, gives a positive indication that characters are *at least* reaching your modem. Besides assisting in the interfacing procedure, this feature also gives a limited test of the digital portions of the modem.

The third useful feature, usually found on higher-priced modems, is a loop-back self-test feature. These tests internally connect a modem's transmitter with its receiver. When a character arrives at the modem's **txd** pin 2, its bit pattern is converted to the appropriate (originate or receive) tones, and, without ever being injected into the telephone lines, these tones are sent immediately to the modem's own receiver. Here the tones are converted back to the original bit pattern, which are then output on the **RxD** pin 3. Even though this feature behaves exactly as the echo feature described above, it differs in that the tone generators and tone receivers are included in the loop-back test.

MODEM INTERFACING CASE STUDY 1: KAYPRO COMPUTER DC HAYES SMARTMODEM 1200 (SN:462124261)

General Considerations

This KayPro is the same unit used in Case Study 3 (Chapter 9).

The Hayes Smartmodem 1200, shown in Figure 12.2, is a 1200/300 baud (i.e., Bell 212A-type), auto-answer, auto-dial, auto-everything modem. The Smartmodem was not chosen just for its programmability or automatic features, but because it is a superb product and, one suspects, a preview of what all modems will be in a few years. That many of its features have already become standards is evinced by the proliferation of imitative products; all, of course, claim to be "Smartmodem compatible." The Smartmodem was also selected because it is universally supported by commercial communications (terminal emulation) software.

The Smartmodem possesses both indicator lamps and an auto-echo mode, but not a loop-back test.

Figure 12.3 shows the chart of the logic level of both devices.

From our experience in Case Study 3 in Chapter 4, we already know that the KayPro is a DTE with an active **cts** input pin 5. Its **RTS** pin 4 is inhibited.

As always, our first task is to be sure that the KayPro is sending data. Screen output is routed to the serial port with the command **STAT LST: = TTY:**. Next, the asserted **DTR** pin 20 is used to pull up the **cts** pin 5, thereby enabling the KayPro's handshaking input. A control-P followed by the CP/M command **DIR** causes a directory listing to scroll across the screen at the KayPro's default data rate, 300 baud. The KayPro side of the interface is now ready to send data to the Smartmodem. (If we wished to use the Smartmodem at 1200 baud, we could switch the KayPro to 1200 using the **BAUD.COM** utility supplied with the computer. As soon as a command is sent to the Smartmodem, it will figure out the KayPro's baud rate and automatically change its own baud rate to match.)

The Smartmodem itself is obviously a DCE: pin 3 is the transmitter, **CTS** is an asserted output and **dtr** is an input. Pin 8, **DCD** (**RECEIVED LINE SIGNAL DETECT**) is inhibited because the Smartmodem does not yet "hear" a modem's idle transmitter on the telephone line. When the Smartmodem connects with another modem, we'll expect **DCD** to become asserted. An inhibited **DSR** pin 6 is somewhat unexpected. **DSR** is intended to signal that the modem is powered up and ready to go.

DTE: KAYPRO   DCE: HAYES SMARTMODEM

TEST RESULTS			I/O	PIN #	I/O	TEST RESULTS
		NEG	!	2 TxD	?	X
		X	?	3 RxD	!	NEG
		NEG	!	4 RTS	?	X
ACTIVE		X	?	5 CTS	!	POS
	(DIMLY)	POS	?	6 DSR	!	NEG
		X	?	8 DCD	!	X
		POS	!	20 DTR	?	X

Figure 12.3: A beginning logic chart for the KayPro and Smartmodem

Following our usual procedure, the next step is to get the modem to accept the KayPro's data. The pin 2's are therefore connected. But how will we know that the Smartmodem is receiving the data? This is where indicator lamps come in handy: when **DIR** is typed the lamp labeled **SD** (for "sent data") flashes to confirm that KayPro's data is arriving at the modem.

The only way to make an outgoing call with the Smartmodem is by sending instructions as part of the data stream. (Its ability to work from codes instead of switches is why it's so "smart.") As long as the Smartmodem is not in a data link, prefixing a telephone number with the code "ATDP" will cause the Smartmodem to dial the number. (If you have a touch-tone phone, use "ATDT.") The Smartmodem contains a small loudspeaker to allow you to hear the numbers as they are dialled. It is not necessary to have the modem connected to the phone line at this time. Use your own telephone number as a test, and be sure to use *only capital letters* in the command.

Unfortunately, when **ATDT8488233** is typed (followed by a carriage return, of course), the modem's **SD** indicator flashes as before, but nothing else happens.

Something must be disabling the Smartmodem. Time to get out the the tester and bag of tricks. The only possible active inputs are **rts** pin 4 and **dtr** pin 20. Both are enabled by jumpering them to **CTS** pin 5. Figure 12.4 shows the state of the interface now.

As the jumper between **CTS** pin 5 and **dtr** pin 20 is applied, the indicator lamp on the front panel marked **TR** (**T**erminal **R**eady) illuminates. The **TR** lamp apparently monitors the state of the **dtr** pin 20 input. Since it would be pointless to monitor an inactive input, we can assume that the modem's **dtr** pin 20 is active.

When **ATDT8488233** is typed again, the Smartmodem springs to life as first a dial tone, then touch tones, and finally a busy signal is heard through its speaker. Removing the trick from **rts** pin 4 has no effect upon the Smartmodem's operation.

The basic task of interfacing the Smartmodem to the KayPro is complete. All that remains is to verify that the modem will successfully establish a data link with another modem. We must also confirm that the Smartmodem will convert incoming data and pass it along to the computer via its RS-232-C interface.

First, let's confirm that it will connect with another modem on the other end of the telephone line. But where can we find another modem to call? If you have a college or university nearby, its computer sciences department will almost certainly maintain one or more modem, or *dial-up* lines. Since you cannot log in to their computer without a password, the information operator will unhesitatingly give you the phone number. There may be different numbers for 300 and 1200 baud.

A sure way to locate a modem is to call one of the large telecommunications networks, Telenet or Tymnet. These networks provide nation-wide networking through local telephone numbers in many cities. Do *not* dial the following numbers with a Smartmodem. These numbers reach a human, whom you may ask for the access number nearest you:

TELENET   TYMNET
(800) 336-0437   (800) 336-0149
(800) 572-0408 (Virginia)

Use the Smartmodem to dial the number you have chosen. Although it is unnecessary, you may include the customary phone number punctuation. You will hear the Smartmodem dial the number.

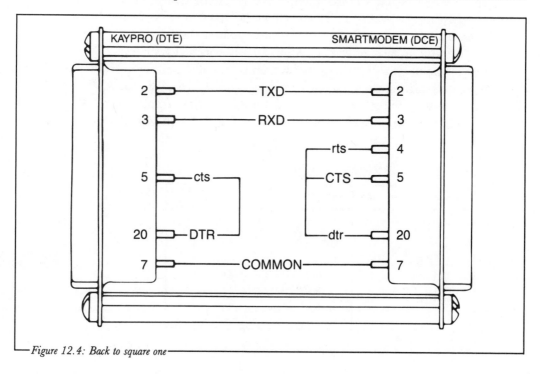

Figure 12.4: Back to square one

When the phone is answered, you will hear the line-idle tone (the "carrier" tone). As soon as the Smartmodem recognizes this tone, the speaker will become silent and the **CD** (carrier detect) lamp will illuminate.

You have now established a data link with a modem on the other end. Figure 12.5 shows the logic levels on the Smartmodem's RS-232-C interface when a data link is established.

As expected, **DCD** pin 8 is now asserted. Notice that **DSR** pin 6 is also asserted. Pins 6 and 8 are apparently internally connected. This use of **DSR** is eccentric and potentially dangerous. **DSR** is generally used to indicate that the modem is powered up and ready. On the Smartmodem, however, this line is not asserted until a data link is established. This will cause problems with software that expects a more conventional **DSR**; the program and the modem will become locked in a deadly embrace—the software requiring **DSR** before it will dial, and the Smartmodem waiting for a data link before asserting **DSR**. Since **CTS** pin 5 is always asserted, it can be used as substitute for the conventional **DSR** signal.

Keep your eye on the Smartmodem's **RD** (received data) lamp. Depending upon the system you have reached, the **RD** lamp may flash to indicate that the other modem is transmitting data bound for your terminal. If the lamp has not flashed within a few seconds of your seeing the **DC** lamp illuminate, the remote system is probably waiting for you to make the first move. Send one or two carriage returns. The **RD** lamp should flash as the other end begins to send data. At present, we unfortunately have no way to display the incoming data—in CP/M

DCE: HAYES SMARTMODEM DURING DATA LINK

PIN #	I/O	TEST RESULT
2 TxD	?	X
3 RxD	!	NEG
4 RTS	?	X
5 CTS	!	POS
6 DSR	!	POS (WITH DATA LINK)
8 DCD	!	POS (WITH DATA LINK)
20 DTR	?	X

Figure 12.5: Smartmodem during data link

there is no easy way to direct incoming serial data to the screen while simultaneously dispatching keystrokes to the serial port. These are the functions of terminal emulator software.

Specify The Cable

We have successfully interfaced the Smartmodem to the KayPro's CPM. Three alternative interfaces are shown in Figure 12.6, 12.7 and 12.8.

This is the "hypothetical" interface we described in Chapter 3. Here, the Smartmodem is restrained from action unless the KayPro's **DTR** output is asserted—that is, unless the KayPro is turned on. This prevents the Smartmodem from automatically answering your phone unless the computer is ready.

In Figure 12.7, you see a slightly more elaborate interface.

Here we have substituted the Smartmodem's **CTS** output where one would expect to find **DSR**. Although it uses different pins, this interface now performs the conventional device control that is "supposed" to take place on **DSR**: unless the modem is turned on, the KayPro will not transmit serial data to it.

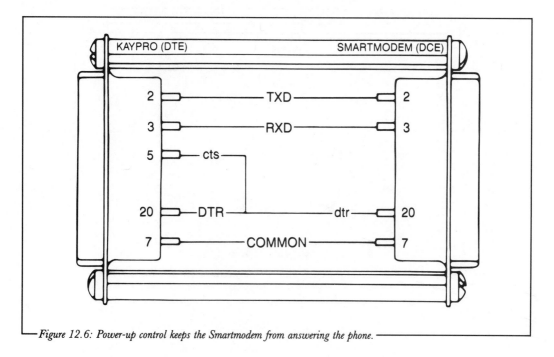

Figure 12.6: Power-up control keeps the Smartmodem from answering the phone.

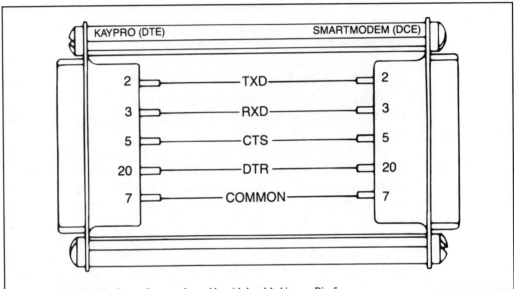

Figure 12.7: The KayPro to Smartmodem cable with handshaking on Pin 5

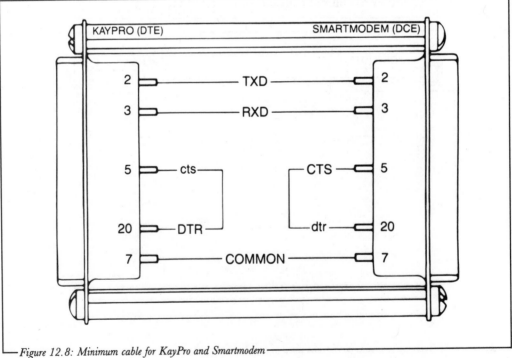

Figure 12.8: Minimum cable for KayPro and Smartmodem

As always, the value of power-up handshaking functions (such as those shown in Figures 12.6 and 12.7) must be weighed against the expense, bulk, and inconvenience incurred by the connection of additional wires to the cable. Figure 12.8 shows the Spartan version of the interface.

COMMENTS

The Smartmodem contains internal microswitches, one of which automatically pulls up its **dtr**. Despite the convenience of these microswitches, it is generally a good idea to include pullups in the cable—this guarantees that the interface will work regardless of the switch settings.

On occasion (as with the Type 'n Talk in Case Study 4), it is useful to begin an interfacing chore by applying null modems. This, however, is one area where a null modem would get you into *big* trouble. Figure 12.9 shows why.

On the Smartmodem side, pin 20 (**dtr**) and pin 6 **DSR** are jumpered with the idea that the **DSR** asserted at power-up will enable the **dtr** input. As we have just seen, however, the normal condition of the Smartmodem's **DSR** is merely to duplicate the **DCD** pin 8 output—normally inhibited. Since it is impossible for a call to be in progress when the Smartmodem is powered up, **dtr** will never become enabled—another deadly embrace!

An almost identical peril exists on the KayPro side. Notice that the null modem connects the **RTS** output on pin 4 with the **cts** pin 5 input. Since **cts** pin 5 is the KayPro's handshaking input, it must be pulled up; but the KayPro's **RTS** pin 4 is *negative!* Jumpering these two pins would entirely prevent the flow of data from the KayPro. The success of null modem devices (cables or adaptors) depends upon a standard implementation of RS-232-C rules; as we have seen, this presumption is not likely to be true with micros. A single input out of place (as with the Type 'n Talk), one normally-positive output inhibited (as with the KayPro or Smartmodem)—any of these conditions will cause the null modem to fail. Moreover, when handshaking is required, the null modem will almost certainly pull up (and therefore defeat) an active input on one side of the interface or the handshaking output on the other.

Three of the interfaces in our case studies were hobbled by the application of null modem cables. Nevertheless, on particularly recalcitrant equipment, a null modem may provide meaningful, if sometimes negative evidence from which to deduce the correct interface configuration. Moral: when nothing else seems to make sense, try a null modem . . . something will probably happen to get you started in the right direction.

INTERFACING MODEMS TO INTELLIGENT TERMINAL SOFTWARE

In the previous chapter, we argued in favor of operating system-level, hardware handshaking for printers. Such an interface is desirable because it "installs" the printer as a permanent resource known to the operating system—in CP/M, this resource's name is **LST:**.

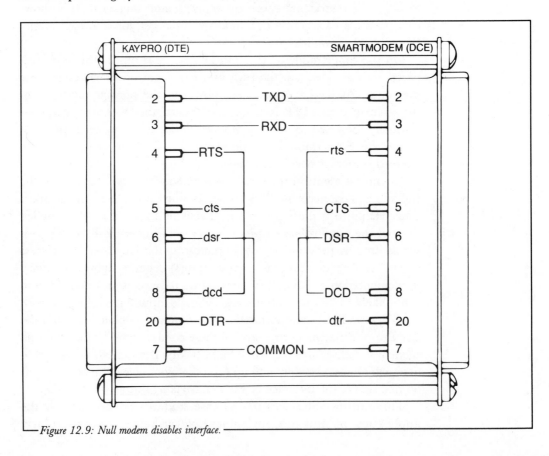

Figure 12.9: Null modem disables interface.

Unfortunately, there is no similar CP/M resource named, say, **MOD:** through which the system may perform serial I/O with devices such as modems.

This is precisely why the KayPro-Smartmodem interface just devised is not particularly useful. To be sure, there are a few applications—for example, modeming text files to a remote printer or computer—where such low-level modem interface might come in handy, but without terminal software the KayPro-Smartmodem combination will not find many applications.

While terminal software is sometimes included with micros, these programs are usually just *dumb terminal* programs capable only of displaying incoming characters on the screen and dispatching keyboard characters to the modem.

Anyone seriously involved with data communications will eventually purchase an *intelligent terminal* or *communications* program. This software provides not only the ordinary dumb terminal functions, but also a wealth of other features: incoming data can be stored on disk files, unwanted characters can be filtered from a data stream, phone numbers are automatically dialled, files can be transferred with error-checking, files can be output in any number of popular text formats, etc. The scope of these features is boundless, restrained only by the imagination of the user.

Communications software is usually unconcerned with the physical details of the device to which the data is transmitted and from which it is received. The program dispatches its data to a UART which in turn sends the data to an RS-232-C port. Inbound data is likewise fetched from a UART. Thus communications software regards I/O much like we regard a post office: none of the machinations of the postal service affect the content or form of the letters we drop off and pick up there.

In the past, communications software has required a user to manipulate the controls of the modem separately from the software. The convenience and automated features of intelligent modems such as the Hayes Smartmodem, however, revealed new horizons for software. Formerly mechanical tasks—such as dialing a phone number, correctly setting the modem to "originate" or "answer" mode, and switching on the modem at just the right time—are all now handled by intelligent modems. With the responsibility of operating the modem thus assigned to the communications software instead of the user, the world of telecommunications is open to countless thousands of souls who would otherwise have been intimidated by its machinery.

Accordingly, much recent communications software is built around intelligent modems. One of the best of these programs is M.I.T.E. (Mycroft Labs, Inc., P.O. Box 6045, Tallahassee, FL 32301). Because of the interesting way in which it interacts with the Smartmodem, and because many of its features will doubtless be imitated by others, M.I.T.E. is a perfect case study. For the sake of continuity, we will still use the KayPro as our sample computer.

We begin, as always, by again cabling the Smartmodem to the KayPro in the most general way possible. In addition to connecting the usual data pins 2 and 3, the Smartmodem's **CTS** pin 5 is used to trick its **dtr** input pin 20. Since we already know that the KayPro's **cts** pin 5 is the active handshaking lead, it must be tricked with a jumper to **DTR** pin 20. Figure 12.10 shows these connections.

After putting M.I.T.E. in the originate mode and telling it what telephone number to dial, the *G* option is selected from the main menu. This choice enters the *terminal mode,* the part of the program that

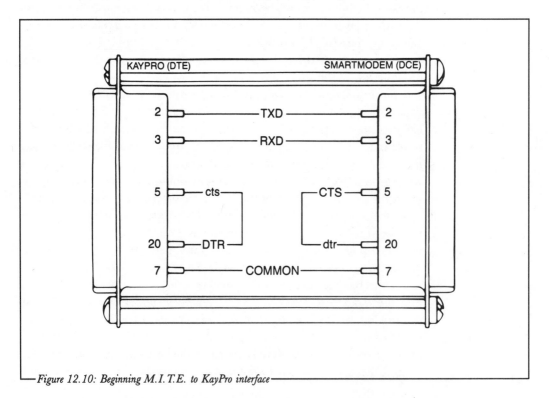

Figure 12.10: Beginning M.I.T.E. to KayPro interface

actually simulates a terminal. After a few seconds, the screen displays:

Now dialing: 836-4911
Awaiting Carrier

Obediently, the Smartmodem begins to beep out the tones. The phone is answered on the other end. The other modem sends its idle tone. The Smartmodem recognizes it and squelches its internal speaker. The **CD** (Carrier Defect) lamp is illuminated and the **RD** (Received Data) lamp flashes to show that M.I.T.E. is now connected to Telenet. We're having fun now!

The carriage return on the KayPro's keyboard is tapped a couple of times to let Telenet know we're alive.

Nothing else happens . . . after 45 seconds or so, M.I.T.E. clears the KayPro's screen and the main menu reappears.

We notice that when other keys are pressed, the (TxD) **SD** lamp does not flash—keyboard characters are not reaching the Smartmodem. Nor was the sign-on message from Telenet displayed on the screen. But the KayPro is obviously sending data—it was able to send the dial command to the Smartmodem. The dialing procedure is repeated, but this time with the LED tester attached to pin 3, just to be sure that the Smartmodem is actually transmitting Telenet's sign-on characters to the KayPro. The flashing of both red and green LEDs confirms it. We must conclude that after it sends the dialing instructions to the Smartmodem, the KayPro will neither send *nor* receive data. What's going on?

Time to snoop around on the KayPro side of the interface. Figure 12.11 shows the KayPro's logic chart while M.I.T.E. is displaying the main menu.

But wait, can this be the KayPro chart? The KayPro has always had that strange inhibited **RTS** output and an asserted **DTR** output. This chart is just the opposite—**RTS** is asserted and **DTR** is now inhibited. This discovery illustrates an important point made earlier: the UART controls the pins on the interface and the *software controls the UART*. The only plausible conclusion is that M.I.T.E. has *initialized* the UART to suit its own need. In a very real sense, then, we are now interfacing the Smartmodem not only to the KayPro, but also to M.I.T.E.

Since this is essentially a new and therefore unknown interface, we must figure it out anew. We know that M.I.T.E. is going to make the

KayPro behave like a terminal and we know from Case Study 1 (Chapter 8) that we can verify terminal operation easily with a data loop-back (jumpering Txd pin 2 and RxD pin 3). We will know we have conquered the KayPro when characters typed on the keyboard are dispatched out pin 2, looped back to the KayPro's receiver on pin 3, and then displayed on the screen.

We mustn't make any assumptions about this new interface, so we'll apply the standard tricks to the two DTE inputs. Since **dsr** pin 6 is, as always, dimly positive (i.e., internally pulled up), it can be ignored for now, but later we'll want to make sure that it's still inactive. The negative **DTR** pin 20 we will also ignore for the time being. Figure 12.12 shows the tricked interface.

Once again, starting from the main menu, the G option is chosen. When the interface was initially tried, the message "Awaiting carrier" was displayed. This time, however, M.I.T.E. displays the following message:

Now resuming previous call

A few keys on the KayPro are pressed. They are immediately printed on the screen. M.I.T.E.'s terminal mode is clearly now working. But what did we change on the KayPro side since the first try? Aside from the data loop-back, only **dcd** pin 8 has been altered. This hypothesis is easily proven by repeating the dialing procedure and, while the **Awaiting carrier** message is displayed, pulling up the KayPro's **dcd** pin 8 with a jumper to **RTS** pin 4.

When this connection is made, the KayPro obligingly beeps and the screen display changes as shown in Figure 12.13.

DTE: KAYPRO

PIN	#	I/O	TEST RESULTS	
2	!	TxD	NEG	
3	?	RxD	X	
4	!	RTS	POS	
5	?	CTS	X	
6	?	DSR	POS	(DIMLY)
8	?	DCD	X	
20	!	DTR	NEG	

———*Figure 12.11: KayPro's interface logic levels with M.I.T.E at main menu*———

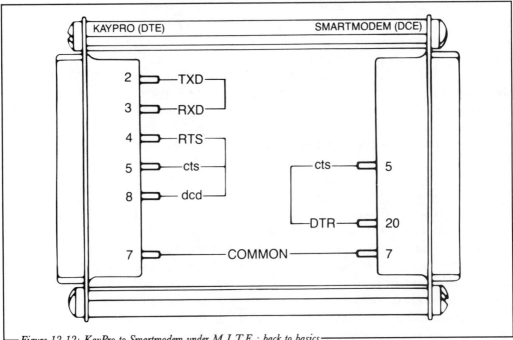

Figure 12.12: KayPro to Smartmodem under M.I.T.E.: back to basics

Now Dialing: 836-4911
Awaiting carrier

      < = = = = =**dcd** to **RTS** jumper applied here

Carrier Detected

Now Dialing: 836-4911
Awaiting carrier

      < = = = = =**dcd** to **RTS** jumper applied here

Carrier Detected

      < = = = = =**dcd** to **RTS** jumper removed here

Carrier lost
Type <CR> to continue

Figure 12.13

This makes immanent sense—M.I.T.E. refuses to commence communications until the Smartmodem has achieved a data link with another modem. When M.I.T.E. detects that **dcd** pin 8 has been enabled, it knows that the Smartmodem has established a data link; M.I.T.E. then permits normal character I/O to the Smartmodem. If the terminal mode is exited—for example, to execute a menu choice—the phone line is *not* hung up and the data link is not broken. Later, when the terminal mode is re-entered via the *G* option, M.I.T.E. discovers that **dcd** pin 8 is *already* enabled and concludes that a previously-established data link already exists. The message ''Now resuming previous call'' is therefore displayed.

Before connecting the Smartmodem's **DCD** pin 8 to the KayPro's **dcd** pin 8, however, let's complete the analysis of the interface by testing the remaining pins for activity. The **cts** pin 5, formerly the handshaking pin under CP/M, is now inactive. **dsr** pin 6 remains inactive.

When the interface is tested with M.I.T.E. in the terminal (as opposed to the menu) mode, the KayPro's **DTR** pin 20 becomes asserted and remains asserted until **dcd** pin 8 is next disabled. In other words, the enabling of **dcd** pin 8 latches **DTR** pin 20 positive. This bit of elegance will take care of the Smartmodem's need for an enabled **dtr**.

Figure 12.14 shows the final, if somewhat cluttered, logic chart for the M.I.T.E./KayPro combo.

DTE: KAYPRO   DCE: HAYES SMARTMODEM

TEST RESULTS		I/O	PIN #	I/O	TEST RESULTS	
	NEG	!	2 TxD	?	X	
	X	?	3 RxD	!	NEG	
	POS	!	4 RTS	?	X	
	X	?	5 CTS	!	POS	
(DIMLY)	POS	?	6 DCD	!	NEG	**
(ACTIVE)	X	?	8 DCD	!	NEG	**
*	POS	!	20 DTR	?	X	(ACTIVE)
*TOGGLES NEG TO POS UPON ENTRY TO TERMINAL MODE **TOGGLES POS WHEN DATA LINK ESTABLISHED						

Figure 12.14: KayPro to Smartmodem final logic chart

It is worth asking, "What happened to the active **cts** input on the KayPro? How did it mechanically become transposed to **dcd** pin 8?" As powerful as it is, M.I.T.E. does *not* rewire the interface, making an active input appear to jump from pin 5 to pin 8. The wires connecting pin 8 and the UART have always been in place. CP/M ignores the logic level on pin 8 while monitoring **cts** instead, but M.I.T.E., is designed to do the opposite. Remember, because the software is always in control, an interface's behavior will vary with the application program. As an illustration of this point, consider that when we exit M.I.T.E., we effectively execute a warm start. But the KayPro's UART remains configured to monitor **dcd** pin 8. This means that the KayPro would not respond to logic changes on **cts** pin 5 and therefore would no longer handshake with the Epson printer used in Case Study 3. A CP/M cold boot is required to reinitialize the KayPro's UART to its default logic states.

SPECIFY THE CABLE

Since this is a DTE/DCE pair, a straight-through cable will work fine. Figure 12.15 shows the final cable.

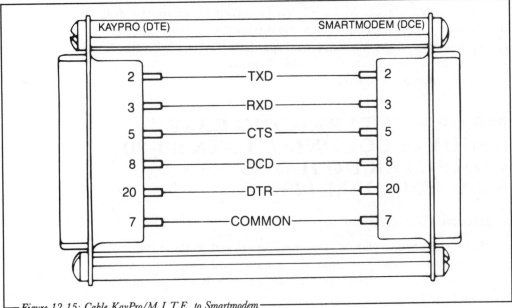

Figure 12.15: Cable KayPro/M.I.T.E. to Smartmodem

COMMENTS

One of the joys of using an intelligent modem is the ability to configure its every nook and cranny to suit personal taste. Ironically, M.I.T.E. doesn't give the user unlimited control of the Smartmodem. Understandably, the Smartmodem does accept commands when in a data link. This sets up a sort of *inverted* deadly embrace: the Smartmodem will not accept commands if its **DCD** is asserted and M.I.T.E. will not allow characters to go to the Smartmodem unless its **dcd** is enabled. There is therefore no way to send your own commands to the modem from the terminal mode.

There are two ways around this problem, neither of them entirely satisfactory. First, a microswitch on the Smartmodem will permanently assert its **DCD** (and, you will remember, its **DSR**) line. This supplies an asserted **DCD** to any program that requires it, independent of the existence of a data link. True, this will fool the software into thinking that a data link is in progress, but M.I.T.E. will no longer auto-dial. Once inside the terminal mode, however, the Smartmodem can be made to dial the number by typing the appropriate command. The point here is that in order to get access to any of the modem's intelligent features, you must sacrifice the built-in auto-dialing.

M.I.T.E. itself offers the second Band-Aid for this problem: through a menu choice, M.I.T.E. can be forced to ignore the **dcd** input. But for the same reason, this also defeats the auto-dial feature.

Lest this seem like a criticism aimed specifically at M.I.T.E., this is a profound weakness in *most* communications software that profess to "support" intelligent modems.

MODEM INTERFACING CASE STUDY 2: COLONIAL DATA SB-80 COMPUTER DC HAYES SMARTMODEM 1200

General Considerations

That the KayPro could be completely interfaced to the Smartmodem was fortuitous. Now that you understand how the Smart modem and M.I.T.E. relate to one another, let's briefly revisit the Colonial Data SB-80.

Let's begin by looking at the SB-80's logic chart in Figure 12.16, which is taken with M.I.T.E. resting at its main menu.

Here, too, M.I.T.E. has changed the character of the interface. The SB-80/M.I.T.E.'s cable to the Smartmodem will look like the cable depicted in Figure 12.17.

DEC: SB-80

PIN	#	I/O	TEST RESULT
2	?	TxD	
3	!	RxD	NEG
4	?	RTS	X
5	!	CTS	POS
6	!	DSR	X
8	!	DCD	NEG *
20	?	DTR	X (ACTIVE)

*TOGGLES POS ON ENTRY TO TERMINAL MODE

Figure 12.16: SB-80 interface logic levels with M.I.T.E. at main menu

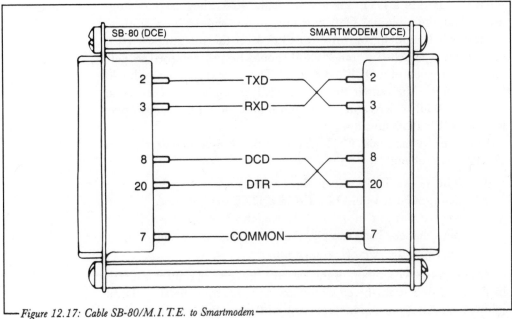

Figure 12.17: Cable SB-80/M.I.T.E. to Smartmodem

COMMENTS

Sometimes people are right for the wrong reasons. Consider the following paragraph:

> In the *standard* DCE arrangement . . . RTS is output to pin 5 and CTS is input from pin 4. DTR is output to pin 8 and DCD is input from pin 20. These may be changed to the *standard* DTE arrangement by simply interchanging the respective pairs.
>
> —*SB-80 User's Manual*

Remember this quotation? Surprise of surprises! It turns out that the **DTR** handshaking signal *is* indeed output from pin 8. **dcd** is *input* from pin 20.

The UART manufacturers are responsible for this apparent absurdity. Although they have absolutely no idea whether any given UART will end up in a DTE or DCE, they insist on assigning RS-232-C standard names to the UARTs' input and output lines. Thus the input line that interrupts the transmitter is usually labeled **CLEAR TO SEND**, while the input that inhibits the receiver is **DATA CARRIER DETECT**. These arbitrary naming conventions work only if the UART is used in a DTE application; with DCEs they are meaningless. What the Colonial Data documentation should have said is, "The UART input (arbitrarily called **dcd** on the integrated circuit data sheet) is attached to pin 20 and should be programmed to perform the function of a DCE's **dtr** line." The second statement should be translated, "the output that the UART manufacturer chooses to refer to as **DTR** is here attached to pin 8 and should be used to perform a DCE's **DCD** function."

In one of its manuals, California Computer Systems attempts to explain this problem:

> The [UART's] control lines were named on the assumption it would be used in a DTE device. Since we are using it in a DCE device, the roles of these pins change. For example, the **DTR** line . . . is connected to the [UART's] **CTS** pin.

Although the recognition of this parallel universe of names is a step in the right direction, the confusion engendered by it persists. Until manual writers (and engineers) deal with this ambiguity, you are likely, from time to time, to conclude that either you or they have gone mad.

CONCLUSION

We have looked at the manner in which a single program manipulates the RS-232-C interface. We could continue with this process, but the conclusion would always be the same—the RS-232-C interface is largely what the software makes of it.

13

TOOLS OF THE TRADE

As your RS-232-C interfacing skill grows, so, miraculously, will your popularity. For some, this popularity will eventually lead to a career as an interfacing guru summoned to exorcize the demons of the DB-25.

Whether you interface professionally or just occasionally for yourself and your friends, you will want to know about some excellent tools designed especially for RS-232-C interfacing. Included in this list are also irresistible gadgets that can streamline your use of serial devices.

BREAKOUT TESTER

Breakout tester is the generic name given to devices that facilitate the interconnection and testing of RS-232-C devices. The name refers to the user's ability to "breakout" specific wires from the cable.

The most basic type is the test header (like those used in our case studies), where two opposite-facing connectors act as a platform for the jumpering and testing of the pins on the interface. This kind of breakout adaptor offers low cost and flexibility. A single unit may be constructed for about $10, or less if the connectors are obtained from a surplus supplier. Because they are simple, they are suited to just about every application. If the jumpers (or grabbers) are replaced with soldered wires, these test adaptors can be permanently installed. On the negative side, the gaggle of grabbers can become cumbersome to use, and sometimes the web of wires between the connectors becomes incomprehensible.

When looking for a more professional test rig, prepare yourself for a shock: price. Even the most rudimentary equipment costs at least three times more than you think it should.

At about $45, the Interconnect Set (Figure 13.1) from Syzygy Computer Systems (482 W Arrow Highway Suite A, San Dimas, CA 91733), shown in Figure 6.1, is just one step up from a simple test header. It consists of male and female DB-25 connectors separated by a circuit board. All 25 pins are connected on the circuit board to a terminal strip containing longer pins that protrude vertically from the board. These longer pins are easily interconnected using the jumper wires supplied. Some of these are **Y** jumpers—that is, they enable a single terminal to be connected to two others. In addition, eight solder holes and corresponding terminal pins are mounted at a blank spot on the printed circuit board; these, together with the regular pins, make virtually any connection possible. Syzygy products are enclosed in a black epoxy half-case, and include sets of #4 hardware for permanent, in-line installation.

Figure 13.1: Photo of Syzygy interconnect set

The Model 232WA (Figure 13.2) wiring adaptor from B&B Electronics (Box 475F, Mendota, IL 61342) is functionally equivalent to the Syzygy Interconnect Set. At only $24.95, its price alone makes it a bargain among overpriced hardware. But it has another clever feature: on one side of the circuit board are the usual long pins to which grabbers can be connected or wires soldered. On the other side of the board is one strip of small sockets for each DB-25 connector into which the jumpers (10 supplied) may be plugged for testing.

Because these strips face each other on standard 0.3-inch centers, they will accept standard printed circuit components. For example, one or two banks of microswitches could be installed on one side of the board for straight-through connections while jumpers are applied on the other side. Like most products from B&B, the 232WA does *not* include mounting hardware or an enclosure.

An interesting variation on the header device theme is the RS-232C DB-25 Pin Reconfiguration Adapter (Figure 13.3) ($60 from Mountain Computer, Inc., 300 El Pueblo Road, Scotts Valley, CA 95066). Instead of using jumpers, this unit effects pin reconfiguration by means of a ten-by-ten matrix of microswitches. The **BIG EIGHT,** plus

—*Figure 13.2: B&B wiring adaptor*—

pins 11 and 25, may be switched. A few solder pads are available for custom application. This is a great idea, but be warned: the switches are *impossible* to use without the reference card. Moreover, the thinking behind the assignment of DB-25 pins to the switch positions is not apparent and probably impossible to commit to memory. It is not obvious how to make certain common connections. For example, to connect the **DTR** pin 20's, each must be separately connected to a third pin (usually 25); this will clearly cause problems if that third pin happens to be active. Despite these problems, it is a well-made, self-contained device.

The next level of breakout device, the *breakout monitor,* is essentially the same as the the the simple patching units just described. In addition to the standard jumperable pins or plugs, this header unit also connects a LED to TxD, RxD, RTS, CTS, DSR, DCD, and DTR. An auxiliary LED is provided for any pin not having its own monitor LED.

The Syzygy Patch Set (Figure 13.4) is typical of this kind of tester. It is packaged similarly to Syzygy's Interconnect Set, but without the

—*Figure 13.3: Mountain Computer Pin Reconfiguration Adaptor*—

additional eight solder holes and corresponding terminal pins. The unit is supplied with 10 two-pin, 4 three-pin, and 1 four-pin jumper assemblies. The price tag is a steep $120. It is difficult to understand how the addition of just eight LEDs and their associated components (even the current-limiting diodes used in the Patch Set) can add more than $70 to the cost of their Interconnect Set.

B&B Electronic's offering in this area, the RS-232 MULTI-ADAPTOR, shown in Figure 13.4, contains monitor LEDs for the **BIG EIGHT** pins and two spares. Employing pins and plugs on opposite sides of the board like B&B's 232WS, the Multi-Adaptor's most unusual feature is a third connector, a female DB-25. The ability to plug in another device might come in handy when trying to debug, say, a printer interface. The computer and printer would be connected as usual; a terminal could be connected into the "tap" in order to display the characters being sent to the printer data or actually to dispatch known characters from the keyboard to the printer. The Multi-Adaptor costs $79.95.

BREAKOUT BOXES

The next level of sophistication in breakout devices is the *breakout box*. Unlike the header units (like the Patch Set or the Multi-Adaptor),

Figure 13.4: Syzygy Test Set

the breakout box is a self-contained tester, complete with hinged cover, and a storage compartment for jumpers. A bank of microswitches allows the user to make all 25 RS-232-C connections straight-through. LEDs monitor the status of important pins.

One of the primary differences among the various brands and models is the manner in which the LEDs are powered. As opposed to LEDs in the header-type monitor that draw current from the RS-232-C interface itself, many breakout boxes use a battery in conjunction with transistor circuitry to supply power to the LED circuitry. Line-powered units have the obvious advantage of economy and portability. But because they are soaking up part of the current that is needed to maintain the correct voltages, they can upset the logic levels on a marginally-functioning interface or cause other misleading results.

The battery-powered LEDs actually extract only a minute amount of current from the RS-232-C interface. This tiny current is then amplified by a transistor and used to drive the LED. Since the actual power required to illuminate the LED comes from the battery, the LED's presence has very little effect on the interface. The drawback of this method lies in the inconvenience of dealing with the batteries.

Paradoxically, the power drain caused by line-powered models can be a boon to the interfacer. For example, when certain inputs are tested, the LED glows more dimly than the others on the interface. This identifies the pin as a pulled-up input, instead of an errant output. Outputs, though, are a different matter. A dim output usually marks a weakened output, one that is potentially marginal with temperature, or that might be incapable of supplying the necessary voltage level to the inputs connected to it. (The value of the 470 ohm resistor in our LED tester was intentionally selected to "load down" the interface in this way.)

A very important consideration is the kind of LEDs used in the breakout box. Although two-color LEDs have been available for years, they have found their way into suprisingly few products. Yet they are a natural for RS-232-C testing equipment. Although most breakout boxes provide a spare LED that can be wired "backward" to indicate negative voltages, this seems an unnecessarily laborious step, one all too likely to be omitted or forgotten. Consider, for instance, the inhibited **DTR** on the KayPro when at M.I.T.E.'s main menu. That green LED stood out like a lighthouse; a dark one would probably have gone unnoticed. Without being conscious of it, we may have muttered "inhibited **DTR** . . . very unusual . . . got to keep an eye on it . . . ." Take into consideration also the importance the green LED plays in ascertaining the sex of an interface. Certainly this can be done by reversing the polarity of the red LED, but it's neither so dramatic nor so much fun.

The best-known of the breakout boxes is the Blue Box (Figure 13.5, Model 60, $159), from International Data Sciences (7 Wellington Road, Lincoln, RI 02865). Twelve LEDs monitor the **BIG EIGHT** plus pins 15,17,21,22,25 and two spares (one of each polarity) are provided. Jumpering is done with the three one-wire and one three-wire assemblies included. The Model 60 is a transistorized, battery-powered unit. Rechargeability is an option. Straight-through connections are made with 24 microswitches. The unit, housed in a blue polypropylene case, is 5 × 3 3/4 × 1 3/4 inches. Batteries are included.

Inmac (2465 Augustine Drive, Santa Clara, CA 95051) offers its battery-powered RS-232 I/O Tester (369-1VN). Twelve single-color LEDs monitor the usual lines. Both male and female connectors are on ribbon cables. Aside from its price of $200, there seems little to distinguish it from other units.

If you prefer a line-powered breakout box, the BLACK BOX CORP's (Box 12800, Pittsburgh, PA 15241) SAM + (Model TS250, Figure 13.6) is worth looking at. It supplies fixed line-powered LED monitors for the **BIG EIGHT** and four spares, of which two are wired backwards to indicate negative voltage. Twenty-four microswitches provide quick straight-through configuration. Jumpering is accomplished by plugging ordinary 24 AWG wires into small sockets. Although only two sockets are provided for each pin, there are four groups of three internally-connected "floating" sockets for making multiple connections. Four straight wires and one Y are included. The TS250 is only slightly larger than a package of cigarettes and comes in a husky steel case. The price is $159. Optional carrying case, $6.

Besides single-colored LEDs, most breakout boxes have another annoying characteristic: their LEDs monitor only one side of the interface. When two devices are connected simultaneously, it is difficult to ascertain which device is the source of a given logic change. During the charting of an interface, therefore, only one device may be plugged in at any time.

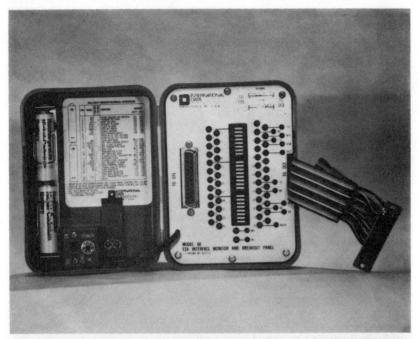

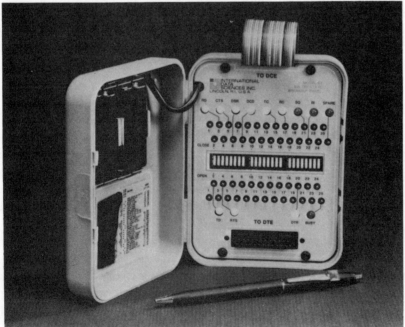

Figure 13.5: Both models come with lifetime guarantees.

The IDS model 61 overcomes both these objections. Twelve two-colored LEDs are used in an intelligent configuration. On the DTE side of the interface, LEDs monitor the three outputs **TxD**, **RTS**, and **DTR**. On the DCE side, **RxD**, **CTS**, **DSR**, **DCD** and pins 15, 17, 22, and 25 are monitored. The Model 61 sells for $265.

The Quick Sly Fox Jumped Over The Lazy Brown Dog

At the far end of the spectrum are the programmable message generators such as the BLACK BOX CATALOG's Fox Box (Model TS150, $455). Hand-held and battery-powered, this unit will actually

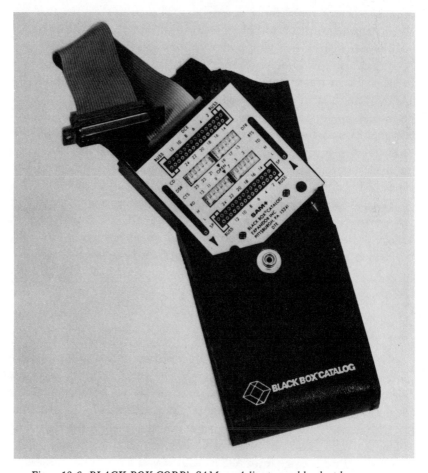

——Figure 13.6: BLACK BOX CORP's SAM + : A line powered breakout box——

transmit one of sixteen messages using any baud rate from 50 to 9600 baud or data format (parity, word size, and framing bits). The messages may contain as many as 128 characters and are user-programmable by means of an erasable programmable read-only memory chip (EPROM). The unit may be changed from DTE to DCE with a single switch and four switch-selectable LEDs monitor the output pins.

Build-It-Yourself Breakout Box

BYTE's "Ciarcia's Circuit Cellar" for April, 1983 is titled, "Build an RS-232-C Breakout Box." Actually, two different breakout boxes are described: a line-powered, one-colored version and a more elaborate, battery-powered two-colored one. The author claims that the former can be constructed for about $15, but $30 is more likely unless you have a well-stocked junk box or can buy everything surplus.

Included in this same article are details for construction of a simple serial character transmitter and receiver. This device will transmit a single character of your choice; it will display a single received character on its two seven-segment displays. Sixteen baud rates are available and common data formats are supported. Be forewarned that characters for transmission are entered as hexidecimal ASCII values; similarly, received characters are displayed as two hexidecimal characters. The letter "M,"for example, would be entered and displayed as "4D."

These devices are constructed upon perforated project boards, but experienced builders should be able to move the circuits onto an etched printed circuit board and into a suitable enclosure.

Neither of these projects is recommended for beginners.

CABLE ACCESSORIES

Sex Reversers

All of the suppliers listed above sell *sex reversers,* also sometimes inaccurately referred to as *gender reversers* or *double sex adaptors.* Sex reversers are needed when two connectors of the same sex come together. Each device consists of a small circuit board with connectors of the same sex on both ends. All twenty-five pins are connected straight-through. The whole assembly is housed in a plastic or epoxy case and supplied with hardware. Prices range from $25 to $30. If you are willing to sacrifice the case and the hardware, B&B Electronics sells sex reversers for $20, or two for $35.

Twelve-inch sex change cables are also available from Inmac. Because all 25 conductors are included in the shielded cable, the cable is quite stiff. If such "pig-tails" are used on the rear of your equipment, they may prevent it from being pushed close to a wall, so use them only between free cables.

Universal Cables

Sex reversers can be eliminated if you purchase a universal cable. These odd-looking cables are made possible by ribbon cable and *insulation displacement connectors* that require no soldering or crimping. As the connector is pressed over the ribbon cable, small metal tines penetrate the insulation on each conductor in the ribbon. Each of these tines become connected to a pin on the DB-25 connector. Because connector installation is a matter of pressing, not soldering or crimping, the

Figure 13.7: Sex changers/null modems

connectors can be installed in the middle of the ribbon just as easily as at the ends.

In Chapter 6, it was recommended that you construct three test adaptors and two male/female cables to accommodate all possible combinations of connectors. If a universal cable is substituted for one of the male/female cables, a single male/female test adaptor will suffice. Prices range from $30–$75. BLACK BOX CATALOG's BOB-232-M/F, shown in Figure 13.9, combines a simple test header with a universal cable. Although it doesn't contain LEDs or switches, its $49.95 price makes this model a tempting buy.

Null Modems

Null modems are available from all these suppliers at about the same price and in the same packages as sex reversers. Null modems generally cause more trouble than they cure, but they occasionally come in handy during troubleshooting. Use them cautiously on devices that handshake.

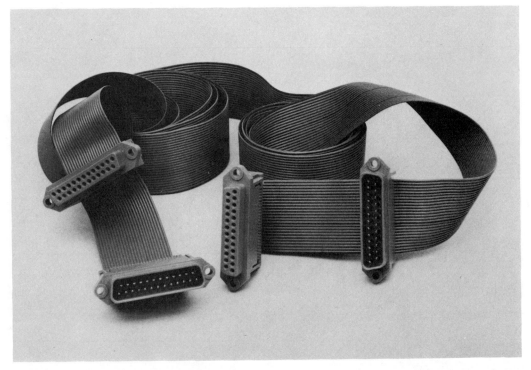

Figure 13.8: Syzygy's universal cable

Switch Boxes

Few gadgets are handier than RS-232-C switch boxes. If you have a modem, a printer, or perhaps a second computer, but your computer has only one serial port, the switch box will enable you to select them one at a time without plugging and unplugging. Because it allows you to switch your device-under-test back and forth between other equipment, a switch box can be a great interfacing aid. Switch boxes are sold by many suppliers, but by far the two best values are from MFJ Enterprises (921 Louisville Road, Starkville, MS 39759).

An almost unbelievable buy at $80, the Model MFJ-1240, Figure 13.10, switches a single input to one of two outputs. Ten pins are switched—2,3,4,5,6,8,11,15,17, and 20. Of these ten, LEDs mounted on the front panel monitor TxD, RxD, RTS, CTS, DSR, CDC, and DTR. As an added bonus, a pushbutton on the front panel reverses pins two and three.

The Model MFJ-1241 (not shown) has all the features of the MFJ-1240, but with one powerful bonus—it not only allows you to switch

Figure 13.9: BLACK BOX CATALOG's BOB-232-M/F

between two peripherals, it permits switching between two computers. Price: $99.95.

Both units are extremely well made, using printed circuit construction throughout and carry a limited one-year guarantee.

Giltronix (3780 Fabian Way, Palo Alto, CA 94303) manufactures a full line of RS-232-C switch boxes. Their two-way device, GRS 232S8AB ($99), switches the **BIG EIGHT** plus pin 22. Add $45 for LED monitors on six lines: Txd, RxD, RTS, CTS, DSR, and DTR.

Parallel-to-Serial Converter

Convert your Centronics parallel port to an RS-232-C port with the Model 775 ($89) from Engineering Specialties (1501-5 Pine Street, Oxnard, CA 93030). The unit plugs directly into the parallel receptacle on your computer, so no modification of your computer is required.

Intelligent Cables

An award for the most unusual accessory goes to the SC-821 Smart Cable from IQ Technologies (1181 N.E. First Street, Suite 308, Bellevue, WA 98005). The Smart Cable automatically interfaces two unknown RS-232-C devices. While looking at the status of two LEDs

—Figure 13.10: The MFJ-1240: Buy it before the manufacturer comes to his senses. —

labeled "M" and "T," simply move a two-position slide switch. When both LEDs are illuminated, the interface is working, complete with handshaking. The only job left to the operator is to make sure that both devices are set to the same data rates and formats. The SC-821 is installed in the center of a universal cable, making it compatible with any combination of DB-25 connectors. In addition, LEDs monitor RTS, CTS, DSR, and DTR at one end. The SC-821 (Figure 13.10) costs $175.

If you are skeptical about the Smart Cable, you are in good company. But it does work. The manufacturer reckons it will function 98 percent of the time. While this claim is impossible to verify, it should be noted that the Smart Cable successfully interfaced the Type 'n Talk to several different computers. IQ Technologies will be happy to supply a list of equipment that stumps the Smart Cable. A smaller version, the SC-817, sells for $95.

At first, the Smart Cable appears to be the ultimate RS-232-C interfacing device, replacing even the most sophisticated breakout boxes. But upon consideration, the Smart Cable is little help with either the occasional interfacing needs of a casual computer user, or the day-to-day problems faced by professional interfacers. The

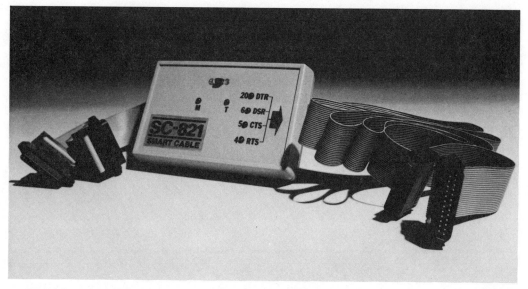

Figure 13.11: IQ technology's SC-817 Smart Cable

Smart Cable *becomes* a working cable—it does not tell you how to *make* a working cable. The Smart Cable does not divulge the internal connections required to complete the interface. While it does an admirable job of correctly connecting data and handshaking leads, the Smart Cable effectively defeats device control signals on its way to finding the handshaking lines. For example, when the KayPro II was connected to a Hayes Smartmodem 1200 that needed an enabled **dtr**, the Smart Cable could not figure it out. It would also be useless in applications (such as the Smartmodem/M.I.T.E. in the last chapter) where software instead of hardware logic drives the interface. It will be useful to computer dealers or equipment sales representatives who must demonstrate their products on a wide variety of equipment. A retail store, for example, would find the Smart Cable a godsend when a customer requests to see how computer X performs with printer Y.

BIBLIOGRAPHY

Barden, William. "Data Communications," *Popular Computing,* (May 1982), 114–118.

Describes data communications: what it is, how it works, and what equipment is needed. Covers data paths, RS-232-C standard, telephone linking, networking, bulletin boards, service networks, and transfer of data over long distances.

Ciarcia, Steve. "Build an RS-232-C Breakout Box," *BYTE,* (April 1983), 28.

An ambitious construction article. Also includes plans for both a stepped-voltage indicator and a terminal simulator.

Davies, T.K. "Build A 'Quick Fox' Terminal Tester," *Kilobaud Microcomputing,* (June 1981), 104–109.

Describes how to construct a "black box" that will continuously send ASCII characters to test a serial I/O board, how to troubleshoot a video terminal, and how to adjust a teletypewriter. Includes a schematic diagram and five photos.

De Jong, Marvin. "Computer Communications Experiments," *Compute!,* (March 1981), 28–33.

Describes how to build an RS-232-C interface that can be used to transmit and receive data over telephone lines. Also includes a program that allows two people to communicate over telephone lines using 6502-based computers.

Hughes, Lawrence. "Introduction To Data Communications," *Microsystems,* (May/June 1981), 29–33.

Explains the communications program used to illustrate software interfacing ideas in Chapter 5. Written by the author of

M.I.T.E., presents a general overview on data communications. Covers TTL link, current loop link, RS-232-C, asynchronous and synchronous serial transmission, simplex, half and full duplex, terminals, and modems.

Folts, Harold C. *McGraw-Hill's Compilation of Data Communications Standards.* New York: McGraw-Hill Publications Co., 1982.

Glossbrenner, Alfred. *The Complete Handbook of Personal Computer Communications: Everything You Need to Go Online with the World.* New York: St. Martin's Press, 1983.

As evinced by the hyperbolic title, this is a gee-whiz book about using a computer and a modem. While there is almost nothing useful in it for interfacing, it is included here because it gives the basic procedures for using Telenet and Tymnet.

Haar, Robert. "Build a Null Modem," *BYTE,* (February 1981), 198.

A modest project extolling the virtues of null modems but none of their dangers.

Leibson, Steve. "The Input/Output Primer, Part 4: The BCD and Serial Interface," *BYTE,* (May 1982), 202.

An excellent series of articles, with a good combination of theory and practice.

Liming, Gary. "Data Paths," *BYTE,* (February 1976), 32.

An early *BYTE* issue, hard to find. Describes basic concepts such as serial and parallel.

McNamara, John E. *Technical Aspects of Data Communication.* Bedford, Mass: Digital Press, 1977.

A thorough, undisguised technical treatment of most aspects of data communication. An excellent book, but probably won't be intelligible unless you understand electronics.

Nichols, Elizabeth A., et al. *Data Communications For Microcomputers.* New York: McGraw-Hill, 1982.

A half-baked engineering book, pawned off as a "microcomputer" user book. Written by engineers with an engineering point of view, its examples lack relevance for most microcomputer applications.

Osborne, Adam. *An Introduction to Microcomputers, Vol. 1* (2nd ed.), Berkeley: Osborne/McGraw-Hill, 1980, 5–94.

Contains a fair description of general I/O and a functional UART.

Parsons, Thomas. "How Data Travels," *Kilobaud Microcomputing,* (October 1981), 46–57.
> Presents an introduction to the mechanics of how data in a computer or terminal is transmitted to another computer. The discussion covers full and half duplex, transmission rates, RS-232-C standard, modems, and types of transmission.

Tugal, Dogan and Tugal, Osman. *Data Transmission,* McGraw Hill, 1981.

Witten, Ian H. "Welcome to the Standards Jungle," *BYTE,* (February 1983), 146.
> Recommended reading. Contains an excellent brief overview of the formal device control logic described by the RS-232-C standard. Discusses the newer serial interface standards.

MISCELLANEOUS:

"EIA Standard RS-232-C: Interface Between Data Terminal Equipment and Data Communication Equipment Employing Serial Binary Data Interchange," Washington, DC: Electronic Industries Association Engineering Dept., 1981.
> This is the RS-232-C standard itself.

BLACK BOX CORPORATION Catalog, Box 128000, Pittsburgh, Pa. 15241.
> This catalog offers a broad array of interfacing tools and data communication equipment. The catalog is a gold mine—a must for amateur and professional alike.

All About Modems. Datapro Research Corp., 1805 Underwood Blvd, Delran, NJ 08075.
> This is an exhaustive shopper's reference guide to modems. It catalogs manufacturers, modem types, and contains an interesting discussion on how to choose a modem for a particular application.

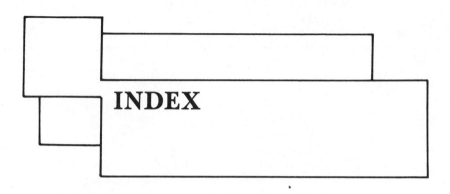

INDEX

Selections from The SYBEX Library

Buyer's Guides

THE BEST OF TI 99/4A™ CARTRIDGES
by Thomas Blackadar

150 pp., illustr., Ref. 0-137

Save yourself time and frustration when buying TI 99/4A software. This buyer's guide gives an overview of the best available programs, with information on how to set up the computer to run them.

FAMILY COMPUTERS UNDER $200
by Doug Mosher

160 pp., illustr., Ref. 0-149

Find out what these inexpensive machines can do for you and your family. "If you're just getting started . . . this is the book to read before you buy."—Richard O'Reilly, Los Angeles newspaper columnist

PORTABLE COMPUTERS
by Sheldon Crop and Doug Mosher

128 pp., illustr., Ref. 0-144

"This book provides a clear and concise introduction to the expanding new world of personal computers."—Mark Powelson, Editor, *San Francisco Focus Magazine*

THE BEST OF VIC-20™ SOFTWARE
by Thomas Blackadar

150 pp., illustr., Ref. 0-139

Save yourself time and frustration with this buyer's guide to VIC-20 software. Find the best game, music, education, and home management programs on the market today.

SELECTING THE RIGHT DATA BASE SOFTWARE
SELECTING THE RIGHT WORD PROCESSING SOFTWARE
SELECTING THE RIGHT SPREADSHEET SOFTWARE
by Kathy McHugh and Veronica Corchado

80 pp., illustr., Ref. 0-174, 0-177, 0-178

This series on selecting the right business software offers the busy professional concise, informative reviews of the best available software packages.

Introduction to Computers

OVERCOMING COMPUTER FEAR
by Jeff Berner

112 pp., illustr., Ref. 0-145

This easy-going introduction to computers helps you separate the facts from the myths.

COMPUTER ABC'S
by Daniel Le Noury and Rodnay Zaks

64 pp., illustr., Ref. 0-167

This beautifully illustrated, colorful book for parents and children takes you alphabetically through the world of computers, explaining each concept in simple language.

PARENTS, KIDS, AND COMPUTERS

by Lynne Alper and Meg Holmberg

208 pp., illustr., Ref. 0-151

This book answers your questions about the educational possibilities of home computers.

THE COLLEGE STUDENT'S COMPUTER HANDBOOK

by Bryan Pfaffenberger

350 pp., illustr., Ref. 0-170

This friendly guide will aid students in selecting a computer system for college study, managing information in a college course, and writing research papers.

COMPUTER CRAZY

by Daniel Le Noury

100 pp., illustr., Ref. 0-173

No matter how you feel about computers, these cartoons will have you laughing about them.

DON'T!
(or How to Care for Your Computer)

by Rodnay Zaks

214pp., 100 illustr., Ref. 0-065

The correct way to handle and care for all elements of a computer system, including what to do when something doesn't work.

YOUR FIRST COMPUTER

by Rodnay Zaks

258 pp., 150 illustr., Ref. 0-045

The most popular introduction to small computers and their peripherals: what they do and how to buy one.

INTERNATIONAL MICROCOMPUTER DICTIONARY

120 pp., Ref. 0-067

All the definitions and acronyms of micro-computer jargon defined in a handy pocket-sized edition. Includes translations of the most popular terms into ten languages.

FROM CHIPS TO SYSTEMS: AN INTRODUCTION TO MICROPROCESSORS

by Rodnay Zaks

552 pp., 400 illustr., Ref. 0-063

A simple and comprehensive introduction to microprocessors from both a hardware and software standpoint: what they are, how they operate, how to assemble them into a complete system.

Personal Computers

ATARI

YOUR FIRST ATARI® PROGRAM

by Rodnay Zaks

150 pp., illustr., Ref. 0-130

A fully illustrated, easy-to-use introduction to ATARI BASIC programming. Will have the reader programming in a matter of hours.

BASIC EXERCISES FOR THE ATARI®

by J.P. Lamoitier

251 pp., illustr., Ref. 0-101

Teaches ATARI BASIC through actual practice using graduated exercises drawn from everyday applications.

THE EASY GUIDE TO YOUR ATARI® 600XL/800XL

by Thomas Blackadar

175 pp., illustr., Ref. 0-125

This jargon-free companion will help you get started on the right foot with your new 600XL or 800XL ATARI computer.

ATARI® BASIC PROGRAMS IN MINUTES

by Stanley R. Trost

170 pp., illustr., Ref. 0-143

You can use this practical set of programs without any prior knowledge of BASIC! Application examples are taken from a wide variety of fields, including business, home management, and real estate.

Commodore 64/VIC-20

THE COMMODORE 64™/VIC-20™ BASIC HANDBOOK
by Douglas Hergert
144 pp., illustr., Ref. 0-116
A complete listing with descriptions and instructive examples of each of the Commodore 64 BASIC keywords and functions. A handy reference guide, organized like a dictionary.

THE EASY GUIDE TO YOUR COMMODORE 64™
by Joseph Kascmer
160 pp., illustr., Ref. 0-129
A friendly introduction to using the Commodore 64.

YOUR FIRST VIC-20™ PROGRAM
by Rodnay Zaks
150 pp., illustr., Ref. 0-129
A fully illustrated, easy-to-use introduction to VIC-20 BASIC programming. Will have the reader programming in a matter of hours.

THE VIC-20™ CONNECTION
by James W. Coffron
260 pp., 120 illustr., Ref. 0-128
Teaches elementary interfacing and BASIC programming of the VIC-20 for connection to external devices and household appliances.

YOUR FIRST COMMODORE 64™ PROGRAM
by Rodnay Zaks
182 pp., illustr., Ref. 0-172
You can learn to write simple programs without any prior knowledge of mathematics or computers! Guided by colorful illustrations and step-by-step instructions, you'll be constructing programs within an hour or two.

COMMODORE 64™ BASIC PROGRAMS IN MINUTES
by Stanley R. Trost
170 pp., illustr., Ref. 0-154
Here is a practical set of programs for business, finance, real estate, data analysis, record keeping and educational applications.

GRAPHICS GUIDE TO THE COMMODORE 64™
by Charles Platt
192 pp., illustr., Ref. 0-138
This easy-to-understand book will appeal to anyone who wants to master the Commodore 64's powerful graphics features.

IBM

THE ABC'S OF THE IBM® PC
by Joan Lasselle and Carol Ramsay
100 pp., illustr., Ref. 0-102
This is the book that will take you through the first crucial steps in learning to use the IBM PC.

THE BEST OF IBM® PC SOFTWARE
by Stanley R. Trost
144 pp., illustr., Ref. 0-104
Separates the wheat from the chaff in the world of IBM PC software. Tells you what to expect from the best available IBM PC programs.

THE IBM® PC-DOS HANDBOOK
by Richard Allen King
144 pp., illustr., Ref. 0-103
Explains the PC disk operating system, giving the user better control over the system. Get the most out of your PC by adapting its capabilities to your specific needs.

BUSINESS GRAPHICS FOR THE IBM® PC
by Nelson Ford
200 pp., illustr., Ref. 0-124
Ready-to-run programs for creating line graphs, complex illustrative multiple bar graphs, picture graphs, and more. An ideal way to use your PC's business capabilities!

THE IBM® PC CONNECTION
by James W. Coffron

200 pp., illustr., Ref. 0-127

Teaches elementary interfacing and BASIC programming of the IBM PC for connection to external devices and household appliances.

BASIC EXERCISES FOR THE IBM® PERSONAL COMPUTER
by J.P. Lamoitier

252 pp., 90 illustr., Ref. 0-088

Teaches IBM BASIC through actual practice, using graduated exercises drawn from everyday applications.

USEFUL BASIC PROGRAMS FOR THE IBM® PC
by Stanley R. Trost

144 pp., Ref. 0-111

This collection of programs takes full advantage of the interactive capabilities of your IBM Personal Computer. Financial calculations, investment analysis, record keeping, and math practice—made easier on your IBM PC.

YOUR FIRST IBM® PC PROGRAM
by Rodnay Zaks

182 pp., illustr., Ref. 0-171

This well-illustrated book makes programming easy for children and adults.

YOUR IBM® PC JUNIOR
by Douglas Hergert

250 pp., illustr., Ref. 0-179

This comprehensive reference guide to IBM's most economical microcomputer offers many practical applications and all the helpful information you'll need to get started with your IBM PC Junior.

DATA FILE PROGRAMMING ON YOUR IBM® PC
by Alan Simpson

275 pp., illustr., Ref. 0-146

This book provides instructions and examples of managing data files in BASIC. Programming designs and developments are extensively discussed.

Apple

THE EASY GUIDE TO YOUR APPLE II®
by Joseph Kascmer

160 pp., illustr., Ref. 0-122

A friendly introduction to using the Apple II, II plus and the new IIe.

BASIC EXERCISES FOR THE APPLE®
by J.P. Lamoitier

250 pp., 90 illustr., Ref. 0-084

Teaches Apple BASIC through actual practice, using graduated exercises drawn from everyday applications.

APPLE II® BASIC HANDBOOK
by Douglas Hergert

144 pp., illustr., Ref. 0-155

A complete listing with descriptions and instructive examples of each of the Apple II BASIC keywords and functions. A handy reference guide, organized like a dictionary.

APPLE II® BASIC PROGRAMS IN MINUTES
by Stanley R. Trost

150 pp., illustr., Ref. 0-121

A collection of ready-to-run programs for financial calculations, investment analysis, record keeping, and many more home and office applications. These programs can be entered on your Apple II plus or IIe in minutes!

YOUR FIRST APPLE II® PROGRAM
by Rodnay Zaks

150 pp., illustr., Ref. 0-136

A fully illustrated, easy-to-use introduction to APPLE BASIC programming. Will have the reader programming in a matter of hours.

THE APPLE® CONNECTION
by James W. Coffron

264 pp., 120 illustr., Ref. 0-085

Teaches elementary interfacing and BASIC programming of the Apple for connection to external devices and household appliances.

TRS-80

YOUR COLOR COMPUTER
by Doug Mosher
350 pp., illustr., Ref. 0-097
Patience and humor guide the reader through purchasing, setting up, programming, and using the Radio Shack TRS-80/ TDP Series 100 Color Computer. A complete introduction.

THE FOOLPROOF GUIDE TO SCRIPSIT™ WORD PROCESSING
by Jeff Berner
225 pp., illustr., Ref. 0-098
Everything you need to know about SCRIPSIT—from starting out, to mastering document editing. This user-friendly guide is written in plain English, with a touch of wit.

Timex/Sinclair 1000/ZX81

YOUR TIMEX/SINCLAIR 1000 AND ZX81™
by Douglas Hergert
159 pp., illustr., Ref. 0-099
This book explains the set-up, operation, and capabilities of the Timex/Sinclair 1000 and ZX81. Includes how to interface peripheral devices, and introduces BASIC programming.

THE TIMEX/SINCLAIR 1000™ BASIC HANDBOOK
by Douglas Hergert
170 pp., illustr., Ref. 0-113
A complete alphabetical listing with explanations and examples of each word in the T/S 1000 BASIC vocabulary; will allow you quick, error-free programming of your T/S 1000.

TIMEX/SINCLAIR 1000™ BASIC PROGRAMS IN MINUTES
by Stanley R. Trost
150 pp., illustr., Ref. 0-119
A collection of ready-to-run programs for financial calculations, investment analysis, record keeping, and many more home and office applications. These programs can be entered on your T/S 1000 in minutes!

MORE USES FOR YOUR TIMEX/SINCLAIR 1000™
Astronomy on Your Computer
by Eric Burgess
176 pp., illustr., Ref. 0-112
Ready-to-run programs that turn your TV into a planetarium.

Other Popular Computers

YOUR FIRST TI 99/4A™ PROGRAM
by Rodnay Zaks
182 pp., illustr., Ref. 0-157
Colorfully illustrated, this book concentrates on the essentials of programming in a clear, entertaining fashion.

THE RADIO SHACK® NOTEBOOK COMPUTER
by Orson Kellogg
128 pp., illustr., Ref. 0-150
Whether you already have the Radio Shack Model 100 notebook computer, or are interested in buying one, this book will clearly explain what it can do for you.

THE EASY GUIDE TO YOUR COLECO ADAM™
by Thomas Blackadar
175 pp., illustr., Ref. 0-181
This quick reference guide shows you how to get started on your Coleco Adam with a minimum of technical jargon.

YOUR KAYPRO II/4/10™
by Andrea Reid and Gary Deidrichs
250 pp., illustr., Ref. 0-166
This book is a non-technical introduction to the KAYPRO family of computers. You will find all you need to know about operating your KAYPRO within this one complete guide.

Languages

C

UNDERSTANDING C
by Bruce Hunter
200 pp., Ref 0-123
Explains how to use the powerful C language for a variety of applications. Some programming experience assumed.

FIFTY C PROGRAMS
by Bruce Hunter
200 pp., illustr., Ref. 0-155
Beginning as well as intermediate C programmers will find this a useful guide to programming techniques and specific applications.

BUSINESS PROGRAMS IN C
by Leon Wortman and Thomas O. Sidebottom
200 pp., illustr., Ref. 0-153
This book provides source code listings of C programs for the business person or experienced programmer. Each easy-to-follow tutorial applies directly to a business situation.

BASIC

YOUR FIRST BASIC PROGRAM
by Rodnay Zaks
150pp. illustr. in color, Ref. 0-129
A "how-to-program" book for the first time computer user, aged 8 to 88.

FIFTY BASIC EXERCISES
by J. P. Lamoitier
232 pp., 90 illustr., Ref. 0-056
Teaches BASIC by actual practice, using graduated exercises drawn from everyday applications. All programs written in Microsoft BASIC.

INSIDE BASIC GAMES
by Richard Mateosian
348 pp., 120 illustr., Ref. 0-055
Teaches interactive BASIC programming through games. Games are written in Microsoft BASIC and can run on the TRS-80, Apple II and PET/CBM.

BASIC FOR BUSINESS
by Douglas Hergert
224 pp., 15 illustr., Ref. 0-080
A logically organized, no-nonsense introduction to BASIC programming for business applications. Includes many fully-explained accounting programs, and shows you how to write them.

PASCAL PROGRAMS FOR SCIENTISTS AND ENGINEERS
by Alan R. Miller
374 pp., 120 illustr., Ref. 0-058
A comprehensive collection of frequently used algorithms for scientific and technical applications, programmed in Pascal. Includes such programs as curve-fitting, integrals and statistical techniques.

DOING BUSINESS WITH PASCAL
by Richard Hergert and Douglas Hergert
371 pp., illustr., Ref. 0-091
Practical tips for using Pascal in business programming. Includes design considerations, language extensions, and applications examples.

Assembly Language Programming

PROGRAMMING THE 6502
by Rodnay Zaks
386 pp., 160 illustr., Ref. 0-046
Assembly language programming for the 6502, from basic concepts to advanced data structures.

6502 APPLICATIONS
by Rodnay Zaks
278 pp., 200 illustr., Ref. 0-015
Real-life application techniques: the input/output book for the 6502.

ADVANCED 6502 PROGRAMMING
by Rodnay Zaks
292 pp., 140 illustr., Ref. 0-089
Third in the 6502 series. Teaches more advanced programming techniques, using games as a framework for learning.

PROGRAMMING THE Z80
by Rodnay Zaks
624 pp., 200 illustr., Ref. 0-069
A complete course in programming the Z80 microprocessor and a thorough introduction to assembly language.

Z80 APPLICATIONS
by James W. Coffron
288 pp., illustr., Ref. 0-094
Covers techniques and applications for using peripheral devices with a Z80 based system.

PROGRAMMING THE 6809
by Rodnay Zaks and William Labiak
362 pp., 150 illustr., Ref. 0-078
This book explains how to program the 6809 in assembly language. No prior programming knowledge required.

PROGRAMMING THE Z8000
by Richard Mateosian
298 pp., 124 illustr., Ref. 0-032
How to program the Z8000 16-bit microprocessor. Includes a description of the architecture and function of the Z8000 and its family of support chips.

PROGRAMMING THE 8086/8088
by James W. Coffron
300 pp., illustr., Ref. 0-120
This book explains how to program the 8086 and 8088 in assembly language. No prior programming knowledge required.

EXECUTIVE PLANNING WITH BASIC
by X. T. Bui
196 pp., 19 illustr., Ref. 0-083
An important collection of business management decision models in BASIC, including Inventory Management (EOQ),

Critical Path Analysis and PERT, Financial Ratio Analysis, Portfolio Management, and much more.

BASIC PROGRAMS FOR SCIENTISTS AND ENGINEERS
by Alan R. Miller
318 pp., 120 illustr., Ref. 0-073
This book from the "Programs for Scientists and Engineers" series provides a library of problem-solving programs while developing proficiency in BASIC.

CELESTIAL BASIC
by Eric Burgess
300 pp., 65 illustr., Ref. 0-087
A collection of BASIC programs that rapidly complete the chores of typical astronomical computations. It's like having a planetarium in your own home! Displays apparent movement of stars, planets and meteor showers.

YOUR SECOND BASIC PROGRAM
by Gary Lippman
250 pp., illustr., Ref. 0-152
A sequel to *Your First BASIC Program*, this book follows the same patient, detailed approach and brings you to the next level of programming skill.

Pascal

INTRODUCTION TO PASCAL (Including UCSD Pascal™)
by Rodnay Zaks
420 pp., 130 illustr., Ref. 0-066
A step-by-step introduction for anyone wanting to learn the Pascal language. Describes UCSD and Standard Pascals. No technical background is assumed.

THE PASCAL HANDBOOK
by Jacques Tiberghien
486 pp., 270 illustr., Ref. 0-053
A dictionary of the Pascal language, defining every reserved word, operator, procedure and function found in all major versions of Pascal.

APPLE® PASCAL GAMES

**by Douglas Hergert and
Joseph T. Kalash**

372 pp., 40 illustr., Ref. 0-074

A collection of the most popular computer games in Pascal, challenging the reader not only to play but to investigate how games are implemented on the computer.

INTRODUCTION TO THE UCSD p-SYSTEM™

by Charles W. Grant and Jon Butah

300 pp., 10 illustr., Ref. 0-061

A simple, clear introduction to the UCSD Pascal Operating System; for beginners through experienced programmers.

Software and Applications

Operating Systems

THE CP/M® HANDBOOK

by Rodnay Zaks

320 pp., 100 illustr., Ref 0-048

An indispensable reference and guide to CP/M—the most widely-used operating system for small computers.

MASTERING CP/M®

by Alan R. Miller

398 pp., illustr., Ref. 0-068

For advanced CP/M users or systems programmers who want maximum use of the CP/M operating system . . . takes up where our *CP/M Handbook* leaves off.

THE BEST OF CP/M® SOFTWARE

by John D. Halamka

250 pp., illustr., Ref. 0-100

This book reviews tried-and-tested, commercially available software for your CP/M system.

REAL WORLD UNIX™

by John D. Halamka

250 pp., illustr., Ref. 0-093

This book is written for the beginning and intermediate UNIX user in a practical, straightforward manner, with specific instructions given for many special applications.

THE CP/M PLUS™ HANDBOOK

by Alan R. Miller

250 pp., illustr., Ref. 0-158

This guide is easy for the beginner to understand, yet contains valuable information for advanced users of CP/M Plus (Version 3).

Business Software

INTRODUCTION TO WORDSTAR™

by Arthur Naiman

202 pp., 30 illustr., Ref. 0-077

Makes it easy to learn how to use WordStar, a powerful word processing program for personal computers.

PRACTICAL WORDSTAR™ USES

by Julie Anne Arca

200 pp., illustr., Ref. 0-107

Pick your most time-consuming office tasks and this book will show you how to streamline them with WordStar.

MASTERING VISICALC®

by Douglas Hergert

217 pp., 140 illustr., Ref. 0-090

Explains how to use the VisiCalc "electronic spreadsheet" functions and provides examples of each. Makes using this powerful program simple.

DOING BUSINESS WITH VISICALC®

by Stanley R. Trost

260 pp., Ref. 0-086

Presents accounting and management planning applications—from financial statements to master budgets; from pricing models to investment strategies.

DOING BUSINESS WITH SUPERCALC™

by Stanley R. Trost

248 pp., illustr., Ref. 0-095

Presents accounting and management planning applications—from financial statements to master budgets; from pricing models to investment strategies.

VISICALC® FOR SCIENCE AND ENGINEERING

by Stanley R. Trost and Charles Pomernacki

225 pp., illustr., Ref. 0-096

More than 50 programs for solving technical problems in the science and engineering fields. Applications range from math and statistics to electrical and electronic engineering.

DOING BUSINESS WITH 1-2-3™

by Stanley R. Trost

250 pp., illustr., Ref. 0-159

If you are a business professional using the 1-2-3 software package, you will find the spreadsheet and graphics models provided in this book easy to use "as is" in everyday business situations.

THE ABC'S OF 1-2-3™

by Chris Gilbert

225 pp., illustr., Ref. 0-168

For those new to the LOTUS 1-2-3 program, this book offers step-by-step instructions in mastering its spreadsheet, data base, and graphing capabilities.

UNDERSTANDING dBASE II™

by Alan Simpson

220 pp., illustr., Ref. 0-147

Learn programming techniques for mailing label systems, bookkeeping and data base management, as well as ways to interface dBASE II with other software systems.

DOING BUSINESS WITH dBASE II™

by Stanley R. Trost

250 pp., illustr., Ref. 0-160

Learn to use dBASE II for accounts receivable, recording business income and expenses, keeping personal records and mailing lists, and much more.

DOING BUSINESS WITH MULTIPLAN™

by Richard Allen King and Stanley R. Trost

250 pp., illustr., Ref. 0-148

This book will show you how using Multiplan can be nearly as easy as learning to use a pocket calculator. It presents a collection of templates that can be applied "as is" to business situations.

DOING BUSINESS WITH PFS®

by Stanley R. Trost

250 pp., illustr., Ref. 0-161

This practical guide describes specific business and personal applications in detail. Learn to use PFS for accounting. data analysis, mailing lists and more.

INFOPOWER: PRACTICAL INFOSTAR™ USES

by Jule Anne Arca and Charles F. Pirro

275 pp., illustr., Ref. 0-108

This book gives you an overview of InfoStar, including DataStar and ReportStar, WordStar, MailMerge, and SuperSort. Hands on exercises take you step-by-step through real life business applications.

WRITING WITH EASYWRITER II™

by Douglas W. Topham

250 pp., illustr., Ref. 0-141

Friendly style, handy illustrations, and numerous sample exercises make it easy to learn the EasyWriter II word processing system.

Business Applications

INTRODUCTION TO WORD PROCESSING

by Hal Glatzer

205 pp., 140 illustr., Ref. 0-076

Explains in plain language what a word processor can do, how it improves productivity, how to use a word processor and how to buy one wisely.

COMPUTER POWER FOR YOUR LAW OFFICE

by Daniel Remer

225 pp., Ref. 0-109

How to use computers to reach peak productivity in your law office, simply and inexpensively.

OFFICE EFFICIENCY WITH PERSONAL COMPUTERS
by Sheldon Crop
175 pp., illustr., Ref. 0-165
Planning for computerization of your office? This book provides a simplified discussion of the challenges involved for everyone from business owner to clerical worker.

COMPUTER POWER FOR YOUR ACCOUNTING OFFICE
by James Morgan
250 pp., illustr., Ref. 0-164
This book is a convenient source of information about computerizing you accounting office, with an emphasis on hardware and software options.

Other Languages

FORTRAN PROGRAMS FOR SCIENTISTS AND ENGINEERS
by Alan R. Miller
280 pp., 120 illustr., Ref. 0-082
In the "Programs for Scientists and Engineers" series, this book provides specific scientific and engineering application programs written in FORTRAN.

A MICROPROGRAMMED APL IMPLEMENTATION
by Rodnay Zaks
350 pp., Ref. 0-005
An expert-level text presenting the complete conceptual analysis and design of an APL interpreter, and actual listing of the microcode.

Hardware and Peripherals

MICROPROCESSOR INTERFACING TECHNIQUES
by Rodnay Zaks and Austin Lesea
456 pp., 400 illustr., Ref. 0-029
Complete hardware and software interconnect techniques, including D to A conversion, peripherals, standard buses and troubleshooting.

USING CASSETTE RECORDERS WITH COMPUTERS
by James Richard Cook
175 pp., illustr., Ref. 0-169
Whatever your computer or application, you will find this book helpful in explaining details of cassette care and maintenance.

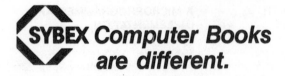

SYBEX Computer Books are different.

Here is why . . .

At SYBEX, each book is designed with you in mind. Every manuscript is carefully selected and supervised by our editors, who are themselves computer experts. We publish the best authors, whose technical expertise is matched by an ability to write clearly and to communicate effectively. Programs are thoroughly tested for accuracy by our technical staff. Our computerized production department goes to great lengths to make sure that each book is well-designed.

In the pursuit of timeliness, SYBEX has achieved many publishing firsts. SYBEX was among the first to integrate personal computers used by authors and staff into the publishing process. SYBEX was the first to publish books on the CP/M operating system, microprocessor interfacing techniques, word processing, and many more topics.

Expertise in computers and dedication to the highest quality product have made SYBEX a world leader in computer book publishing. Translated into fourteen languages, SYBEX books have helped millions of people around the world to get the most from their computers. We hope we have helped you, too.

For a complete catalog of our publications please contact:

U.S.A.
SYBEX, Inc.
2344 Sixth Street
Berkeley,
California 94710
Tel: (415) 848-8233
Telex: 336311

FRANCE
SYBEX
6–8 Impasse du Curé
75018 Paris
France
Tel: 01/203–9595
Telex: 211801

GERMANY
SYBEX-Verlag GmbH
Vogelsanger Weg 111
4000 Düsseldorf 30
West Germany
Tel: (0211) 626441
Telex: 8588163

UNITED KINGDOM
SYBEX, Ltd.
Unit 4–Bourne Industrial Park
Bourne Road, Crayford
Kent DA1 4BZ England
Tel: (0322) 57717
Telex: 896939